Sue Freeman
Rich Freeman '98

By Rich & Sue Freeman

Footprint Press
Fishers, New York, 14453
www.footprintpress.com

Other books available from Footprint Press:

Take a Hike! Family Walks in the Rochester Area
Bruce Trail - An Adventure Along the Niagara Escarpment
Alter - A Simple Path to Emotional Wellness

Published in the United States of America by Footprint Press

Edited by Diane Maggs
Cover by Image & Eye Graphics Services
Maps by Rich Freeman
Pictures by Rich & Sue Freeman

ISBN 0-9656974-2-8

Manufactured in the United States of America

Library of Congress Catalog Card Number: 97-078232

Every effort has been made to provide accurate and up-to-date trail descriptions in this book. Hazards are noted where known. Users of this book are reminded that they alone are responsible for their own safety when on any trail or road and that they ride or walk the routes described in this book at their own risk.

The authors, publishers, and distributors of this book assume no responsibility for any injury, misadventure, or loss occurring from use of the information contained herein.

Dedication

This book is dedicated with our sincere thanks to Rich's parents, Dick and Ginny Freeman. They generously let us live in their home while they were in Florida, which allowed us to continue writing this book and to search for new, future adventures.

Trail Locations by Trail Number

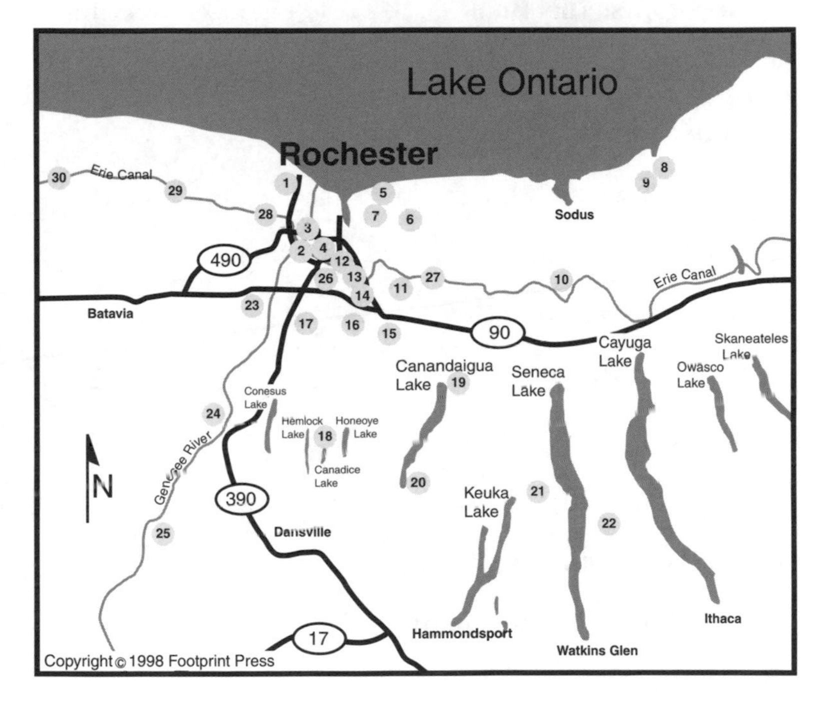

CONTENTS

Contents

Acknowledgments

Rochester and its surrounding counties are a community blessed with civic leaders and private citizens who have preserved our heritage and built the trails described in this book for all of us to enjoy. Through the preservation of abandoned railroad beds and the development of trails along major arteries, they're gradually building a network of trails that will someday crisscross our area. Each year, more miles are opened as the land is secured, brush is cleared, and bridges are built to span our many waterways. The rides described by the maps and guides in this book are works in progress. Each year, more is accomplished by groups such as:

Crescent Trail Association (Joy Barnitz et al)
Friends of Genesee Valley Greenway (Fran Gotscik et al)
Friends of the Outlet (Phil Whitman et al)
Friends of Webster Trails (Jack Kersen et al)
Finger Lakes Trail Conference (Howard Beye et al)
Hansen Nature Center (Ron Walker et al)
Macedon Trail System Associates (Pete Henry et al)
The Mendon Foundation (Carl Foss et al)
Ontario Pathways (Betsy Russell et al)
Pittsford Trails (Victor Yates et al)
Victor Hiking Trails (Dave Wright et al)

To these volunteer organizations we owe a debt of gratitude. Without their hard work and dedication, we wouldn't have trails to ride or walk. We also thank the leaders of these groups for lending their support in the making of this book.

Likewise, it's foresight, planning, and action by our public officials that result in paths dedicated to us bicyclists and outdoors enthusiasts. Kudos and thanks go to:

Cayuga County Office of Tourism (Meg Rogers)
Cayuga County Planning Board (Tom Higgins)
City of Rochester, Bureau of Parks and Recreation (Jim Farr)

City of Rochester, Water and Lighting Bureau (Don Root)
Finger Lakes National Forest Ranger District (Martha, Al, and Kari)
Henrietta Parks Department (Bill Dykstra)
Letchworth State Park (Jayne McLaughlin)
Monroe County Parks Department (Dave Rinaldo)
New York State Thruway Authority
New York State Department of Environmental Conservation
Pittsford Parks and Recreation Department
Town of Greece
Town of Webster
Wayne County Planning Department (Jim Coulombe)
Webster Parks and Recreation Department

Within the Rochester community we have many friends who have shared their knowledge and given assistance in making this book possible. Thank you to: Amy Amish (Image & Eye Graphics Services, cover designer), Rick French (Pack, Paddle, Ski Corp.), Diane Maggs (editor), Dick Spade and Dan Wilson (Adirondack Mountain Club), Seth Irwin and Bill Johnstone (who saved our pictures from an electronic nightmare), Jerry Bond (Cornell Cooperative Extension), and Richard Reisem (local author).

Introduction

If you walk into a bike shop in Rochester and ask where you can go bike riding and be safely off roads, you're likely to hear about the canal towpath, also known as the Erie Canalway Trail, but not much else. That trail is spectacular, and we include it in this book. But, many other options are available around Rochester; they're just a well kept secret. Well, the secret's out! This book is loaded with havens that you can retreat to for a short respite or a long adventure. Choose the length and type of terrain to fit the ability of the participants.

We enjoy bike riding very much. It makes us feel great, it's fun, and it's inexpensive. What a combination! But, we don't particularly like riding the narrow shoulder of a busy road as cars and trucks zip by within inches of our bikes. That's not relaxing, and it's certainly not fun. Biking doesn't have to be like that. Off-road alternatives exist that are much more conducive to a family outing or an invigorating adventure. You'll find them in this book.

The American Heart Association recommends 30 to 60 minutes of physical activity at least 3 to 4 times per week to maintain cardiovascular fitness. You're more likely to achieve this level if you pick activities that you enjoy and that are convenient. Biking is a perfect way to improve the fitness of your heart and lungs. It burns calories too. Here's a breakdown of approximate calorie use per hour for three weight categories:

Persons weight:	100 lb.	150 lb.	200 lb.	
bicycling 6 mph	160	240	312	calories burned per hour
bicycling 12 mph	270	410	534	calories burned per hour

You don't need a special (translation - expensive) bike to enjoy these trails. The only bike that isn't suited to an off-road venture is a road-racing bike. See the section "Types of Bikes" for specifics. The important thing is to grab this guide, hop on your bike, and go for a ride.

And, why stop at bicycling? Many of the trails listed in this book are equally well-suited to hiking, cross-country skiing, bird watching, rollerblading, running, and strolling. Enjoy them at various seasons and using various means of locomotion. Each visit can be a unique experience. CAUTION: If you venture onto the rural trails during the fall hunting season, be sure to wear bright colors so that hunters can spot you easily.

Many of the trails in this book were built by and are maintained by volunteer or community groups. They all welcome new members, especially anyone who is willing to help with the work. We encourage everyone to join a trail group and benefit from the camaraderie and service to your community. All trails listed in this book are free and open to the public. You do not need to be a member of the sponsoring group to enjoy the trails.

If you find inaccurate information or substantially different conditions (after all, things do change), please send a note detailing your findings to: Footprint Press, P.O. Box 645, Fishers, NY 14453.

How To Use This Book

We have clustered the trails into six geographic groups, using downtown Rochester as the center dividing point:

Rides Northwest of Rochester
City Rides
Rides Northeast of Rochester
Rides Southeast of Rochester
Rides Southwest of Rochester
Erie Canalway Trail

The trails range in length from a short 1.2 miles to 85 miles. An index in the back of the book ranks the trails by length so that you can select ones to fit the endurance of your group. Some of the trails are loops, but most, because they are converted railroad beds, are not. But, when you retrace the route, the return trip can often look quite different from your new perspective, even though you're covering the same ground. Or, to add variety, there is always the option of riding one way on the trails and the other on the roads. Some of the trails can be joined to lengthen your ride. Or shorten the ride by turning back at any point along the route or parking a car at one of the alternative parking spots listed.

The riding times given are approximate and assume a moderate pace of 6 to 7 miles per hour. You may find that you travel faster or slower, so adjust the times accordingly. Also, adjust the times to include stops or breaks for resting, eating, observing nature, viewing historical artifacts, and the like. You can easily stretch a two-hour bike ride into an all-afternoon affair if you take time to enjoy the adventure along the way.

We listed some of the amenities you'll find as you travel. After all, when you work hard on a bike ride, you deserve a treat. (You'll quickly find as you read this book that we're ice cream lovers.) We also indicate bike shops that are located near the trails in case you require emergency repairs. Some of the trails are conducive to weekend getaways, so we've listed available camping and nearby bed-and-breakfast accommodations.

Legend

At the beginning of each trail listing, you'll find a map and a description with the following information:

Location: A general description of the town the trail is located in and the endpoints of the trail.

Parking: Where to park to follow the trail as described in the Trail Directions.

Alternative Parking: Other parking locations with access to the trail. Use these if you want to shorten your ride by starting or stopping at a spot other than the designated endpoints.

Riding Time: The approximate time that it will take to bike the trail one way at a moderate pace of 6 to 7 miles per hour, adjusted for the difficulty of the terrain. Add to this "riding time," the amount of time you stop for breaks, sightseeing, or other fun adventures to arrive at the total time needed for any particular outing.

Length: The distance from start to finish of each trek one way.

Difficulty: A description of the amount of elevation change you can expect. Each trail is rated as easy, moderate, or difficult.

Easy = Generally flat, a paved or hard-packed riding surface.

Moderate = Could be hilly or a softer riding surface, so you'll pump those pedals harder.

Difficult = Quite hilly or a rough trail. You'll get an aerobic workout for sure.

Surface: The materials that make up the surface for the majority of the trail.

Trail Markings: Markings used to designate the trails in this book vary widely. Some trails are not marked at all but are cleared or worn paths which you can easily follow. As long as there aren't many intersecting, unmarked paths, you shouldn't lose your way. Other trails are well marked with either signs, blazes, or markers and sometimes a combination of all three. Trail markings are established by the official group that maintains the trail.

Signs - wooden or metal signs with instructions in words or pictures.

Blazes - painted markings on trees showing where the trail goes. Many blazes are rectangular and placed at eye level. Colors may be used to denote different trails. If a tree has twin blazes beside one another, you should proceed cautiously because the trail either turns or another trail intersects.

Markers - small plastic or metal geometric shapes (square, round, triangular) nailed to trees at eye level to show where the trail goes. They also may be colored to denote different trails.

Uses: Each trail has a series of icons depicting the activity or activities allowed on the trail. These include:

Hiking

Bicycling

Dog Walking

Wheelchairs	Rollerblading	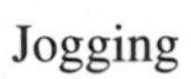 Jogging

Horseback riding	Snowmobiling	Cross-country skiing

Contact: The address and phone number of the organization to contact if you would like additional information or if you have any questions not answered in this book.

MAP LEGEND

Airport

Major Road

Secondary Road

Railroad

Main Trail

Other Trail

Water

Park Boundry

(104) Route #

P Parking

Bridge

Directions

In the directions we often tell you to turn left or right. To avoid confusion in some instances we have noted a compass direction in parentheses according to the following:

(N) = north
(S) = south
(E) = east
(W) = west

Some trails have "Y" or "T" junctions. A "Y" junction indicates one path that turns into two paths. The direction we give is either bear left or bear right. A "T" junction is one path that ends at another. The direction is turn left or turn right.

Guidelines

Any adventure in the outdoors can be inherently dangerous. It's important to watch where you are going and keep an eye on children. Some of these trails are on private property where permission is benevolently granted by the landowners. Please respect the landowners and their property. Follow all regulations posted on signs and stay on the trails. Our behavior today will determine how many of these wonderful trails remain for future generations to enjoy.

Follow "no-trace" ethics whenever you venture outdoors. "No-trace" ethics means that the only thing left behind as evidence of your passing are your footprints and tireprints. Carry out all trash you carry in. Do not litter. In fact, carry a plastic bag with you and pick up any litter you happen upon along the way. The trails included in this book are intended for day trips. Please, no camping or fires.

As the trails age and paths become worn, trail work groups sometimes reroute the trails. This helps control erosion and allows vegetation to return. It also means that if a sign or marker doesn't appear as it is described in the book, it's probably due to trail improvement.

Remember:

Take only pictures, leave only prints.

Please do not pick anything.

History of the Bicycle

For much of man's history on earth, he had two choices for getting around, either on foot or on the back of an animal (such as horses, mules, and wooly mammoths). Bicycles were developed to add another transportation option that multiplied human efficiency by a factor of approximately five. But the history of bicycles is very fuzzy. Sources often disagree as to the names of the inventors and the dates of their inventions. Leonardo DaVinci sketched a facsimile of the modern bicycle in 1490. It was way ahead of its time and, as far as we know, never left the drawing board. Around 1790 a French craftsman named de Sivrac developed a "Celerifere" running machine, which had two in-line wheels connected by a beam. The rider straddled the beam and propelled the Celerifere by pushing his feet on the ground, scooter fashion.

DaVinci's sketch

Celerifere

In 1817 German Baron Karl von Drais added steering. Several versions appeared around France and England by the early 1800s. As a replacement for the horse, these "hobby horses" became a short-lived craze. The roads of the time were too rutted to allow for efficient wheeled transport.

Scottish blacksmith Kirkpatrick MacMillan developed a rear-drive bike in 1839 using a treadle and rod for the rear drive mechanism. But, he lived in the Northern British Isles where people and ideas traveled slowly, so his invention didn't spread. R.W. Thompson patented a pneumatic tube in 1845. Prior to this invention, bikes had metal wheels.

The French anointed Ernest Michaux "father of the bicycle," as he and his brother Pierre added cranks and pedals. Their Velocipede started a bicycle boom. The larger front wheel made it faster but less stable. The war of 1812 brought an end to the French bicycle boom.

Velocipede

British engineers were next to pick up the design and improve upon it by adding ball bearings, pneumatic (Dunlop) tires, wire-spoked wheels, chain drive, variable gears, and cable controls. Over a twenty-year span, the British brought the bicycle to its present form, thanks mainly to James Starley of the Coventry Sewing Machine Company. In 1885 the Starley Rover safety bike was born, returning wheels to a reasonable size and improving the bike's stability.

Safety Bicycle

The bicyling craze began in Rochester around 1880. After practicing in a rented hall, nine brave men hit the streets of Rochester on bicycles. Their endeavors led to formations of the Rochester Bicycling Club, cycling schools, bicycle races, and in 1899, a bicycle festival and parade which attracted a large crowd.

Rochester's first bike path was opened in Charlotte, and the Sidepath Association sold usage licenses for $.25 per year. By 1901 Monroe County had 125 miles of cinder paths for bicycling.

In the early days, women's dress (corsets, pointed shoes, and voluminous skirts) limited their participation in this new sport.

Newspapers of the day railed against the "sorcers" or bicycle speedsters.

Our first famous bicyclist was Rochester native Nick Kaufman, who gathered a chestful of medals on a world tour as a trick cyclist.

Types of Bikes

If you've shopped for a bicycle within the last ten years or so, you know that the choice can be overwhelming. So many types of bikes are available with unfamiliar names like derailleur, cruisers, mountain bikes, BMX, adult ballooners, and coaster-brake bikes. Gear speeds range from 1 to 21 speeds. To ride the trails listed in this book, you don't have to be an expert on bikes or have a specific type of bike. Many of the bikes housed in garages today (and found often at garage sales) are quire suitable on these trails. Let's review the major groups:

10-Speed Bikes

Derailleur bikes are commonly called 10-speed bikes, but they come in 5, 6, 10, 12, 15, or 20 speeds. The derailleur, a French word meaning "to derail," either lifts or pushes the chain from one gear to the next. These bikes are generally lightweight with drop handlebars, hand brakes, no fenders, a narrow saddle, and high pressure tires. Designed to be racing bikes and long-distance pavement bikes, their popularity boomed in the 1970s. Derailleur bikes can be used on any of the paved trails in this book; they are not suited to the non-paved trails.

Single-Speed, Coaster-Brake Bikes

Baby boomers like us have grown up with these bikes. They are heavy bikes with low-pressure balloon tires, wide upright handlebars, a large padded seat, and as the name implies, only one speed. Braking is accomplished by backpedaling. Tough, sturdy work-horses, these bikes last a long time and can take a pounding on the trails listed in this book. Because of the single speed, you may occasionally find yourself walking up a hill. (But we do that anyway even with our 15-speed bikes!)

Cruisers or Adult Ballooners

Internal-hub-geared bikes or cruisers have many features in common with the single-speed, coaster-brake bikes except that they do have gear shifting. The shifting mechanism is contained inside the rear hub and is activated by hand brakes and cables from the handlebars. They come in 2, 3, or 5 speeds. The term "ballooners" derives from their fat, low-pressure tires. They make excellent trail bikes.

BMX Bikes

BMX is an abbreviation for Bicycle Moto-Cross. These tough bikes are mini-ballooners with fat tires originally designed for trick riding both on and off road.

Mountain Bikes

Also called all-terrain bikes (ATB) or hybrids, mountain bikes became the rage of the 1990s. They offer the functionality of a 10-speed bike with the durability of a cruiser. Mountain bikes typically have flat handlebars; heavy-duty brake levers; indexed, thumb-shift levers; wide, knobby tires; heavy-duty rims; and reinforced frames. They're designed to be light weight and strong, as an all-terrain vehicle. Mountain bikes are available in 10, 15, 18, and 21 speeds.

Safety

Regardless of age, everyone who hops on a bike should wear an approved, protective helmet. It's the law in New York State for anyone under the age of 14. Wearing a bicycle helmet significantly reduces the chances of a serious brain injury if you fall off of your bike. Unfortunately, every year nearly 50,000 bicyclists suffer serious head injuries. Many never fully recover, and often the injuries are fatal. Why take the risk when prevention is so simple?

It's important that the helmet fits properly. It should sit level, cover your forehead, and not slide backward. Helmets come in many sizes; select one that feels comfortable and doesn't pinch. Then, use the sizing pads supplied with the helmet for "fine tuning" to achieve a snug fit. Finally, adjust the straps so that they are snug but not pinching. Now you're ready for an enjoyable and safe ride.

Courteous biking can help ensure that trails stay open for bikers. When you're around others, ride to the right in single file. Always signal before passing. It's easy for a bicycle to quickly sneak up on a pedestrian or slower biker and startle them. To avoid this, call out as you approach someone. A simple "on your left" alerts the person to your presence and lets them know which side you're approaching from. When you stop, pull off to the side of the path. Be conscious not to impede the progress of others. Stay on the trails. Do not create or use shortcuts, as they can result in added erosion to the area.

Bicycling with Children

Children love the excitement of bike riding. Add to that new surroundings to explore, and you're sure to have a fun-filled adventure. Ensure a pleasant trip with these simple tips. Plan to take frequent breaks. Carry lots of water and some snacks. Play a game along the way. Read ahead in this guide and assign your child the task of finding the next area of interest. Let your child pick the next break spot. Take time to stop, point out, and discuss things you find on the trail, such as beaver dams, animal tracks, and flowers.

You may have noticed that it's hard to find helmets small enough for an infant. There's a good reason for that. Infants under 12 months of age should not ride in a bicycle child seat, trailer, sidecar, or any other carrier. The fact is that babies are so susceptible to brain injuries that the risks outweigh the rewards. More than a third of the injuries to babies in carriers occur when the bicycle falls over while standing still. So, please wait until your child is a year old before taking him or her along on this enjoyable sport.

Once your child passes the one-year mark, you can begin using a child seat that mounts on the bike's rear wheel. Make sure that the child is wearing an approved helmet and is securely but comfortably belted. The bicycle should have spoke protectors to assure that the child's feet stay out of harm's way. The child seat should be high enough to support the child's head. Remember, when transporting a child in a child seat, your bicycle will require a longer breaking distance, will be less maneuverable, and will swerve if the child shifts suddenly.

A Word about Dogs

Outings with dogs can be fun with their keen sense of smell and different perspective on the world. Many times they find things that we would have passed without noticing. They're inquisitive about everything and make excellent companions. But to ensure that your "outing companion" enjoys the time outside, you must control your dog. Dogs are required to be leashed on most maintained public trails. The reasons are numerous, but the top ones are to protect dogs, to protect other hikers, and to ensure that your pet doesn't chase wildlife. Good dog manners go a long way toward creating goodwill and improving tolerance to their presence.

Most of the trails listed in this book welcome dogs. The only trails which prohibit dogs are:

4. Mount Hope Cemetery
26. Hanson Nature Center Trail

Clothing and Equipment

You don't need much more than a sturdy bicycle and a helmet to enjoy these trails. But here are some tips about clothing to wear and miscellaneous equipment to bring along. Shoes that tie or buckle are best; slip-on shoes could slip off unless they fit snugly. Sandals are not recommended. Sneakers are a good choice.

Dress in layers so that you can peel down as your heart rate rises during the trip. You'll probably have to put the layers back on when you stop for a break. We find it convenient to have a handle-bar bag on the front of our bikes for discarded clothing and other items.

The one accessory that's mandatory is a bottle of water. It's easy to put a bottle holder on your bike or toss a water bottle in a handle-bar bag. Keeping hydrated is important even on a short trip.

Other handy things to have are an energy snack, a tire patch kit and pump, a first-aid kit, a bike lock, insect repellant, sunscreen, a hat, a raincoat, and this guidebook. In summer, if you're biking near water (such as North Ponds Park or Cayuga County Trail), don't forget your swimsuit and towel.

Bike Racks

The first challenge in being able to enjoy the trails listed in this book is getting your bicycle to the trailheads. This often requires some sort of bike rack. Bike racks come in many varieties and many prices. You can spend well over $200 or pick up one inexpensively at a garage sale. Before you head out shopping, think about the following questions to help you select a rack to fit your needs.

1. What vehicle will be used to reach the trailheads?
2. How many bikes will you need to transport?
3. Do the bikes all have quick-release front wheels?
4. Are any of the bikes an unusual size or shape (for example a small child's bike)?
5. Who will load the bicycles on the rack? Are they strong enough to lift the bicycles to the roof?
6. Will you need the extra security of a lockable bike rack?
7. Will the rack be specifically for bikes or do you also need to carry skis or other sports equipment?
8. How often are you likely to use the rack?
9. How much do you want to spend?

No rack is ideal for all vehicles and users. The tradeoffs you make will depend on your situation. For instance, if you plan to use the rack infrequently, you may be willing to tradeoff some ease-of-use for a lower price. Here's some of the variety you'll find as you shop:

- Roof racks attach to the top of a vehicle. It's important to know if your vehicle has gutters or not. Roof racks can be noisy from wind resistance. They require someone with strength to hoist the bicycles to the roof. You have to be careful not to forget that the bicycles are up there and drive into a garage. (We know this from experience!) With some roof racks, you can't open your vehicle's sun roof, however, they do allow full access to your trunk.
- Rear racks mount on the back of a vehicle with brackets and straps. They can scratch paint and can be hard to attach. Most

limit your access to the trunk, but they are generally inexpensive, and you can load bikes quite easily.

- Hitch racks mount on the rear of a vehicle but use a trailer hitch as their main point of attachment. They're less likely to scratch your vehicle but are more expensive.
- Sport trailers are good for carrying many bicycles, but remember that you'll pay extra if you drive on a toll road. These trailers obviously require more storage space.

Rides Northwest of Rochester

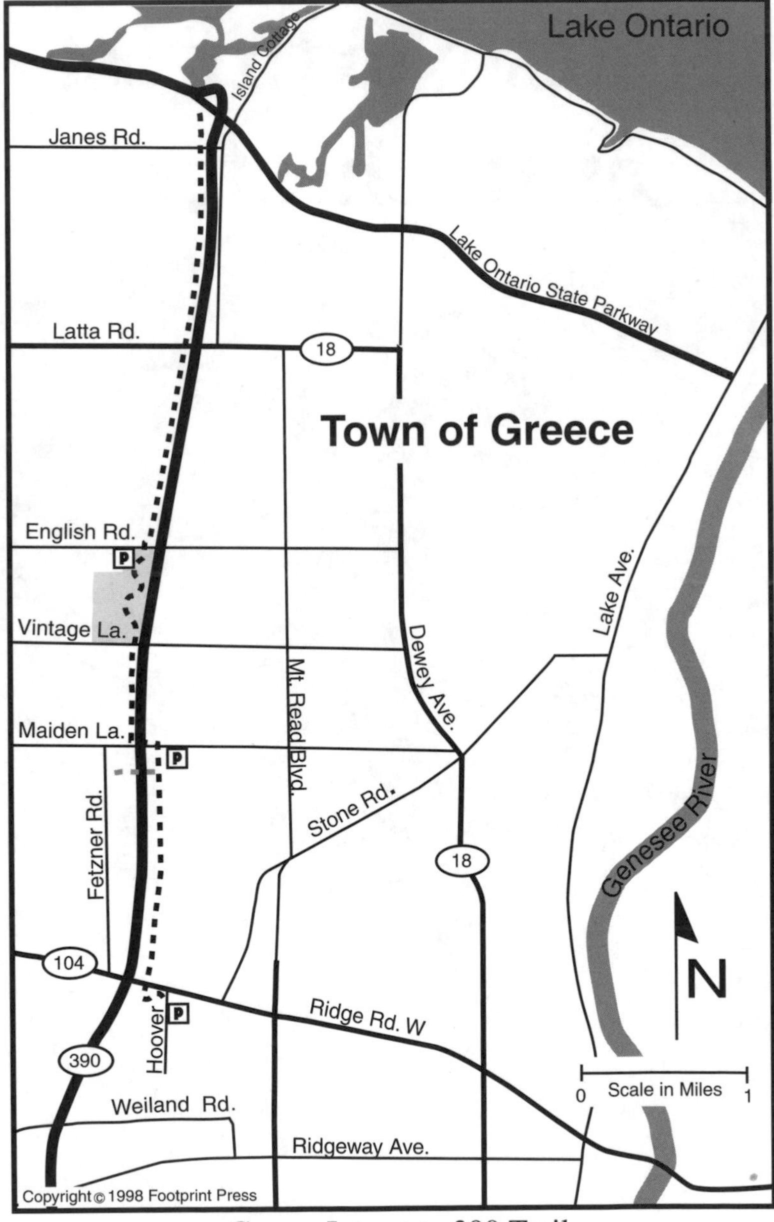

Greece Interstate 390 Trail

1.

Greece Interstate 390 Trail

Location:	Parallel to Interstate 390 from Ridge Road West (Route 104) to the Lake Ontario State Parkway, Greece
Parking:	Greece Odyssey School parking lot on Hoover Drive, just south of the Olive Garden Restaurant on Ridge Road West (Route 104)
Alternative Parking:	Greece Olympia School, Maiden Lane, Greece Basil A. Marella Park, English Road, Greece (across from Parkland School)
Riding Time:	40 minutes one way
Length:	5 miles one way
Difficulty:	Easy, mostly level, some small hills
Surface:	Paved (asphalt)
Trail Markings:	Green-and-white metal signs on posts showing a biker above the numbers 390
Uses:	
Contact:	Town of Greece Department of Human Services 500 Maiden Lane Rochester, NY 14616 (716) 663-0200

The pedestrian and bicycle bridge across busy Route 104.

Enjoying the easy-riding, paved path of the Greece Interstate 390 Trail.

Greece Interstate 390 Trail

This bike path slices through the town of Greece giving the cyclist a sample of its diversity from busy Ridge Road, to suburban backyards, to deep woods, fields, and orchards. On the way you may see rabbits, great blue heron, turtles, and ducks, not to mention the usual birds, squirrels, and chipmunks. The ride north is an easy pedal, but save some energy. Your return will be slightly uphill.

This path is well marked. In addition to metal signs reading "390 biking" on posts, at each crossing you'll see the silhouette of a biker painted on the asphalt. We were debating whether to call this marking "the roadkill biker," but decided against it.

If you haven't expended enough energy by the time you complete this trek, the Greece Odyssey School has a World Trail Fitness Course that you can try while your kids romp in the playground. Or, if you've worked up a monumental hunger, Appleby's, Olive Garden, and Bob Evan's Restaurants await you on Ridge Road.

Bike Shop: The Bike Zone, Creekside Plaza, 771 Fetzner Road, (716) 225-9760

Trail Directions

- From the Greece Odyssey School parking lot, turn right (N) on the sidewalk along Hoover Drive.
- Cross Hoover Drive at the traffic light on the corner of Ridge Road West (Route 104).
- Double back on the opposite side of Hoover Drive and climb the ramp of the large, brown, pedestrian bridge to cross Route 104.
- Bear right off the bridge on the paved bike path as it heads north, parallel to Interstate 390.
- Pass Greece Olympia High School sports fields on your right. (At the school property, a spur to the left goes up a ramp to cross Interstate 390 and end at Fetzner Road.)
- Continue past Greece Olympia High School.
- Turn left at Maiden Lane, under the Interstate 390 bridge.

- Cross Maiden Lane at the crosswalk and continue north. (Note: A bicycle shop called The Bike Zone is in Creekside Plaza on Fetzner Road, just south of Maiden Lane.)
- Pass through woods and beside a creek.
- Cross Vintage Lane.
- Follow the paved path through English Road Park as it winds its way through the woods to Basil A. Marella Park on English Road.
- Cross English Road and bear right.
- Cross Latta Road.
- Pass an apple orchard and cross Janes Road. (Turn right here if you plan to continue on the Ontario State Parkway.)
- Cross a small bridge over a creek.
- At the off-ramp from Ontario State Parkway to Interstate 390, turnaround and reverse your trek. There is no parking at this northern terminus. Heading south you'll notice things you never saw on your northward journey, and you'll get more exercise with the slight uphill rise.

City Rides

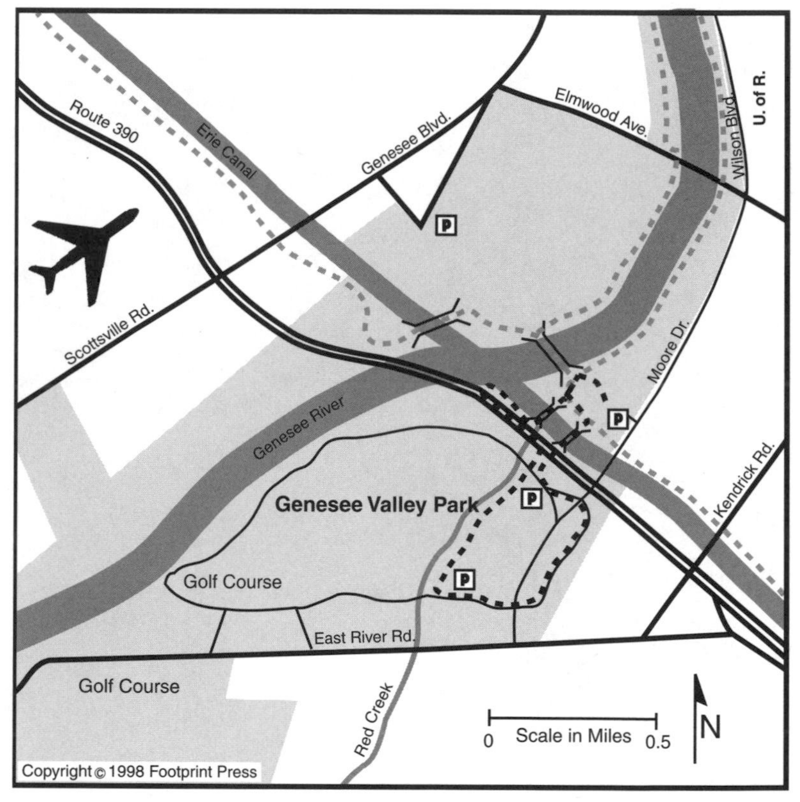

Genesee Valley Park Loop

2.

Genesee Valley Park Loop

Location:	Genesee Valley Park, Moore Drive, Rochester
Parking:	Genesee Valley Park, off Moore Drive, near the Roundhouse Pavilion
Alternative Parking:	Genesee Valley Park off Genesee Street
Riding Time:	20 minutes round trip
Length:	2.6 miles round trip
Difficulty:	Easy, mild hills
Surface:	Paved (asphalt)
Trail Markings:	None
Uses:	
Contact:	Monroe County Parks Department 171 Reservoir Avenue Rochester, NY 14620 (716) 256-4950

This is a fun little loop which meanders over the Erie Canal twice on beautifully arched bridges, under the overpass of Interstate 390, and along Red Creek. It's a short loop with restrooms and picnic pavilions along the way. The hills make it interesting, but the pavement makes it an easy ride. There are four arched bridges over the waterways in this section. Three span the Erie Canal and one spans the Genesee River.

This loop can be connected with the Genesee River - Downtown Loop Trail (#3) or add it to a stretch of the Erie Canalway Trail (#28).

One of three arched bridges over the Erie Canal and Genesee River in Genesee Valley Park.

Genesee Valley Park is one of four Rochester parks designed by famed landscape architect Frederick Law Olmsted. Olmsted's designs were revolutionary for the late 1800s. Instead of laying out precise squares and gardens, he planned clumps of woods, meandering trails, bridle paths, and spectacular views. He planted trees carefully to effect a "forested" look. This natural, quiet ambience was half of Olmsted's design philosophy. The other half was the creation of spaces for more active use, such as open areas for baseball fields, and ponds for swimming in summer and ice skating in winter. Pavilions and bridges designed in a neo-classical style separate activity areas. The other Rochester parks designed by Mr. Olmsted are Seneca Park, Highland Park, and Maplewood Park.

Pat and Don Cushing of Pittsford, NY are wearing flourescent green vests to increase their visibility to others.

Trail Directions

- From the parking lot, head west toward the Genesee River on the paved path.
- Turn left and bear left past the Waldo J. Nielson Bridge which spans the river (do not take this bridge).
- Turn right to cross the next bridge. This takes you over the Erie Canal. You can see arched bridges over the canal in both directions from this vantage point.
- Bear right just before the Interstate 390 overpass.
- The path winds through a wooded area then bends left to loop back between the north and southbound overpasses of Interstate 390.
- Bear right uphill, then turn right after Red Creek onto the paved path.
- Pass the Red Creek pavilion on your left.
- At the park road, turn left.

  (Side trip: At the park road you can turn right and ride to the clubhouse of the Genesee Valley Golf Club, a public course. It offers hots, hamburgers, drinks, and snacks as well as restrooms.)
- Pass the park entrance off East River Road.
- Turn left and pass two pavilions, restrooms, and a third pavilion.
- The paved path ends. Continue straight to Park Drive.
- Turn left and follow the road back to the path leading to the right, under Interstate 390.
- Ride under Interstate 390 and keep right as the path leads over an arched bridge over the Erie Canal.
- After the bridge turn left.
- Keep bearing right on the paved path to return to the parking lot.

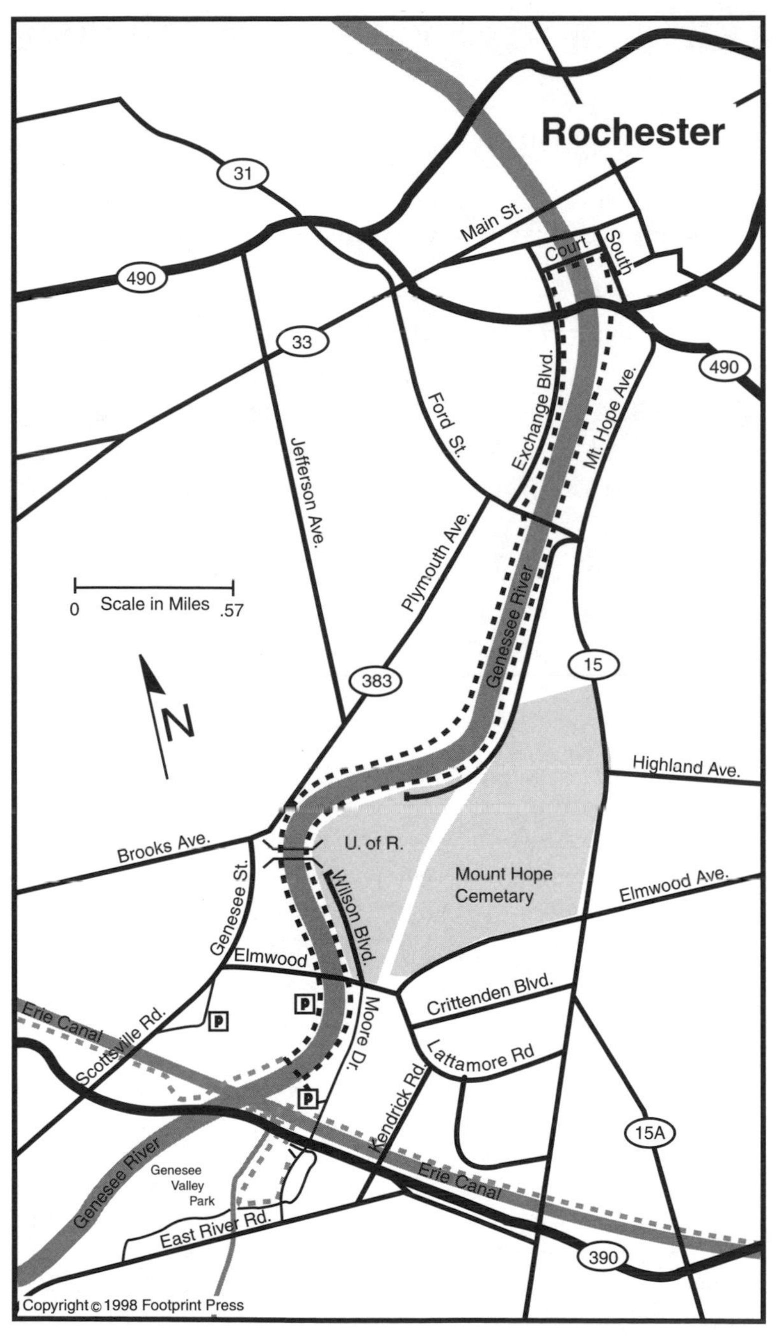

Genesee River - Downtown Loop Trail

3.

Genesee River - Downtown Loop Trail

Location:	Genesee Valley Park through downtown, Rochester
Parking:	Genesee Valley Park, off Moore Drive, near the Roundhouse Pavilion
Alternative Parking:	Rochester Water Sports Center, 145 Elmwood Avenue
	Genesee Valley Park, off Genesee Street
Riding Time:	1 hour
Length:	7-mile loop
Difficulty:	Easy, mostly level
Surface:	Paved (asphalt)
Trail Markings:	A few sporadic signs
Uses:	
Contact:	City of Rochester, Bureau of Parks and Recreation 400 Dewey Avenue Rochester, NY 14613

This wonderful loop trail encompasses the Genesee Valley Park, Genesee River Trails, and sections through the University of Rochester. It takes you along the eastern side of the river heading into downtown and along the western side heading back to Genesee Valley Park. The loop described here is actually a series of trails. Portions of the riverbank trails are maintained by Monroe County, others by the University of Rochester. The Genesee River Trail is maintained by the City of Rochester, Bureau of Parks and

The University of Rochester chapel reflected in the Genesee River.

Recreation. The small section of Erie Canalway Trail is maintained by the New York Thruway Authority. Together they've developed a perfect loop for bike riding.

As we rode, we watched the U of R sculling team practice, while workers hauled trees from the river and piled them on barges. Parts of this path on the west side of the river follow old railroad beds. In downtown you'll pass the original Lehigh Valley train station. In the 1830s, before the railroads, this land held the Genesee Valley Canal, which joined Rochester with the southern tier of New York.

You'll pass through the River Campus of the University of Rochester. Construction of this campus began in 1927 after the University obtained it in a trade with Oak Hill Country Club for a portion of land east of the city. In the thirteenth century, the River Campus lands housed an Algonquin Indian village of bark cabins and farm fields.

The pedestrian bridge that spans the Genesee River has been a crossroads for decades. Rock ledges were exposed on the river bottom in this area during low water, making it a natural site at which to ford. Many Native American trails converged here. In the 1800's a settlement called "Castletown" began on the west bank. Named for the local tavern proprietor, Isaac Castle, Castletown suffered economic ruin when the Erie Canal was routed through the northern town of Rochesterville.

This ride can be shortened by cutting across the Ford Street bridge. To lengthen it, combine it with the Genesee Valley Park Loop (#2) or add it to a stretch of the Erie Canalway Trail (#28). For a true adventure, combine your bike ride with a ride on the boat Sam Patch, or rent a canoe and paddle along the Genesee River.

Genesee River - Downtown Loop Trail

Distances between main roads:

Genesee Valley Park to Ford Street	2.6 miles
Ford Street (east bank) to Court Street	0.7 mile
Court Street to Ford Street (west bank)	1.4 miles
Ford Street (west bank) to Elmwood Avenue	1.7 miles
Elmwood Avenue to parking lot	0.6 mile

Tours: Sam Patch Tour Boat, 12 Cornhill Terrace, (716) 262-5661

Looking north toward downtown Rochester
from along the Genesee River.

Trail Directions

- •From the parking lot, head west toward the Genesee River.
- •Bear right (N) toward the towers of the University of Rochester and Elmwood Avenue.
- •As you approach Elmwood Avenue, bear left to go under the bridge.
- •The path winds back to street level.
- •Pass a river overlook platform.
- •At the University of Rochester information kiosk, bear left, downhill.
- •Pass the back of the University of Rochester chapel.
- •Ride under the pedestrian bridge, then uphill along Wilson Boulevard.
- •Ride under an abandoned railroad bridge.
- •Notice the grand view of downtown Rochester down the river to your left.
- •Pass a residential area, then the Episcopal Church Home.
- •Ride under Ford Street. You are now in Genesee Gateway Park and have ridden 2.6 miles.
- •Ride under Interstate 490, then turn left onto the sidewalk of South Avenue.
- •Turn left onto the sidewalk of Court Street. Pass the Lehigh Valley Railroad station built in 1905. Rundel Library is to your right. You've now ridden 3.4 miles - halfway there!
- •Cross over the Genesee River, then turn left on Exchange Boulevard.
- •Ride under Interstate 490. The Cornhill section of Rochester is on your right across the street.
- •Pass the South River Docking Facility across from the Cornhill Center. This is home to the tour boat Sam Patch.
- •You are now riding parallel to the Genesee River, heading south on the west side of the river.
- •Ride under Ford Street.
- •Pass old factories on your right. You're riding on the old Rochester and Southern Railroad bed.
- •Stay on the paved path as it heads downhill to the woods.

•Eventually, a cement wall parallels the path on the left.
•Emerge from the woods parallel to Plymouth Avenue.
•Pass the University of Rochester pedestrian bridge.
•Bear left onto the asphalt path.
•Bear left at the "Y" to go under Elmwood Avenue.
•Pass the ice rink and Rochester Water Sports Center. Canoe rentals are available here from May 24 until October 5. Parking is available here.
•Proceed uphill on the paved path.
•At the first intersection, turn left. (To extend your ride, travel straight here and take the next left to make a short loop.)
•Turn left and cross the Genesee River on the Waldo J. Nielson Bridge. Mr. Nielson was a leading advocate of converting abandoned railroad beds and towpaths into trails and is responsible for your being able to enjoy this ride today.
•Turn left immediately over the bridge.
•The first right toward the pavilions brings you back to the parking lot.

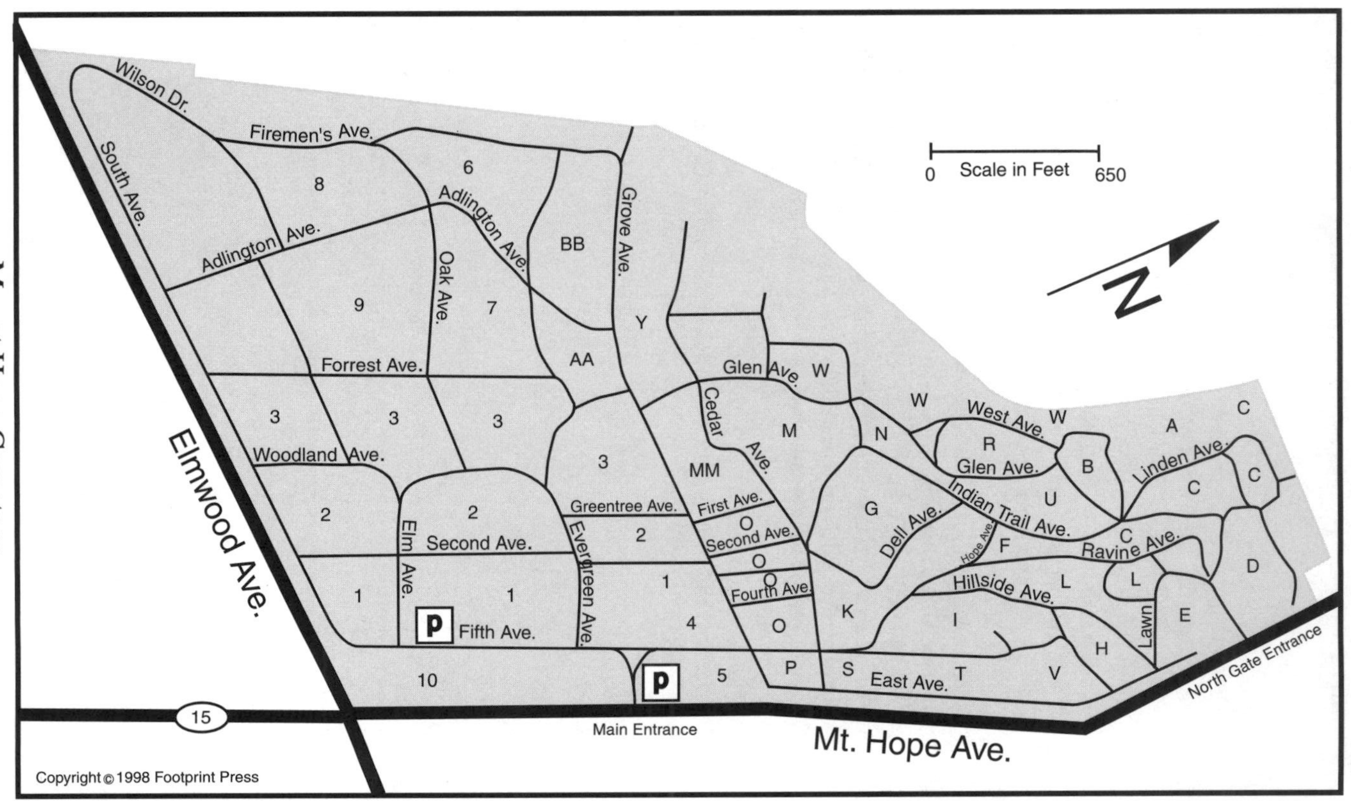

Mount Hope Cemetery

4.
Mount Hope Cemetery

Location:	Elmwood Avenue and Mount Hope Avenue, Rochester
Parking:	In front of the cemetery office just inside the Mt. Hope Avenue entrance
Alternative Parking:	Along Fifth Avenue within the cemetery
Riding Time:	Your choice
Length:	There are 14.5 miles of roads within the cemetery
Difficulty:	Moderate, northern part is hilly
Surface:	Paved (asphalt)
Trail Markings:	Some roads have old road signs. Some corners have cement posts with road names or plot numbers.

Uses: 

Contact: Mount Hope Cemetery
1133 Mt. Hope Avenue
Rochester, NY 14620
(716) 473-2755

If you've never been to Mount Hope Cemetery, you're missing both a historical treasure and a gorgeous landscape. The roads within the cemetery are mostly narrow and paved, and although they are used by cars, the cars drive slowly making it a safe area to bicycle. The southern part of the cemetery is flat, but the northern half is a rugged area sculpted by the glaciers which covered the Rochester area millions of years ago. Mount Hope Cemetery has four large kettles, one of which (Sylvan Waters) is still filled with water. Indian Trail Avenue within the cemetery lies on an esker once used by the Seneca Indians as a major transportation route between the Bristol hills and Lake Ontario.

Kettles were created when a large block of ice separated from a glacier. Water running off the glacier deposited gravel and debris all around the ice block. The block melted, leaving behind a rough circular depression.

Eskers were formed when rivers flowed under the glacier in an ice tunnel. Rocky material accumulated on the tunnel beds, and when the glacier melted, a ridge of rubble remained.

Instead of describing a specific route within the cemetery, we're leaving you free to explore at will and create your own loops. As you can see on the map, there are many possibilities. The exploration and discovery can be part of the fun of visiting Mount Hope Cemetery. Don't worry about getting lost. It's easy to see major landmarks, and many corners are labeled to give you your bearings.

Mount Hope Cemetery

Mount Hope Cemetery was established in 1838 as the first Victorian cemetery in America to be planned, developed, and maintained by a municipality. Before the nineteenth century, people were buried in the woods near villages or next to churches. During the reign of Queen Victoria, a shift in attitude occurred, and death came to be considered a more romantic and celebrated phase of life, defined by the "dust-to-dust" philosophy. This led to a trend toward rural, garden cemeteries called "Victorian cemeteries."

In the 1830s a cholera epidemic hit Rochester and taxed the limits of the community and its church burial grounds. An alternative had to be found. The Rochester Common Council formed a committee to select and purchase land for a cemetery. Despite much dissension, they purchased a 54-acre plot of land one and a half miles from downtown. One of the committee members, General Jacob Gould complained that the land was "all up hill and down dale, and with a gully at the entrance at that." It's the ups and downs that make Mount Hope Cemetery such a beautiful place today.

The newly-purchased land was heavily wooded, and locals called it a howling wilderness because of its resident bears and wolves. The original forest included red, black, and white oak, chestnut, American beech, red and sugar maple, basswood, tulip tree, and white ash. Some of the trees in the cemetery today are well over 300 years old. However, many were cleared to develop burial plots. In 1847 George Ellwanger and Patrick Barry presented a gift of 50 trees from their nursery operation. Their gift included European purple, fernleaf, weeping beech, Nikko fir, Caucasian spruce, Norway maple, and variegated sycamore maple trees.

The cemetery remained unnamed for many months. A laborer named William Wilson submitted his bill using the words "for labor at Mount Hope." The name stuck and was used without any formal adoption. Over the years acreage was purchased piecemeal to increase the size of Mount Hope Cemetery, until today it covers 196 acres.

As you bike among the old trees, you'll see mausoleums, statues, gravestones, and fountains. Many of the people important in Rochester's history are buried here including Susan B. Anthony, Hiram Sibley, John Jacob Bausch, Henry Lomb, Margaret Woodbury Strong, Colonel Nathaniel Rochester, and Frederick Douglass. There are plots of veterans from the Revolutionary War, Civil War, Spanish American War, and both World Wars. To fully understand what you're seeing, we recommend the following book, available at local bookstores and libraries:

Mount Hope - America's First Municipal Victorian Cemetery
Text by Richard O. Reisem
Photography by Frank A. Gillespie
Published by Landmark Society of Rochester, New York
ISBN # 0-9641706-3-9

Rides Northeast of Rochester

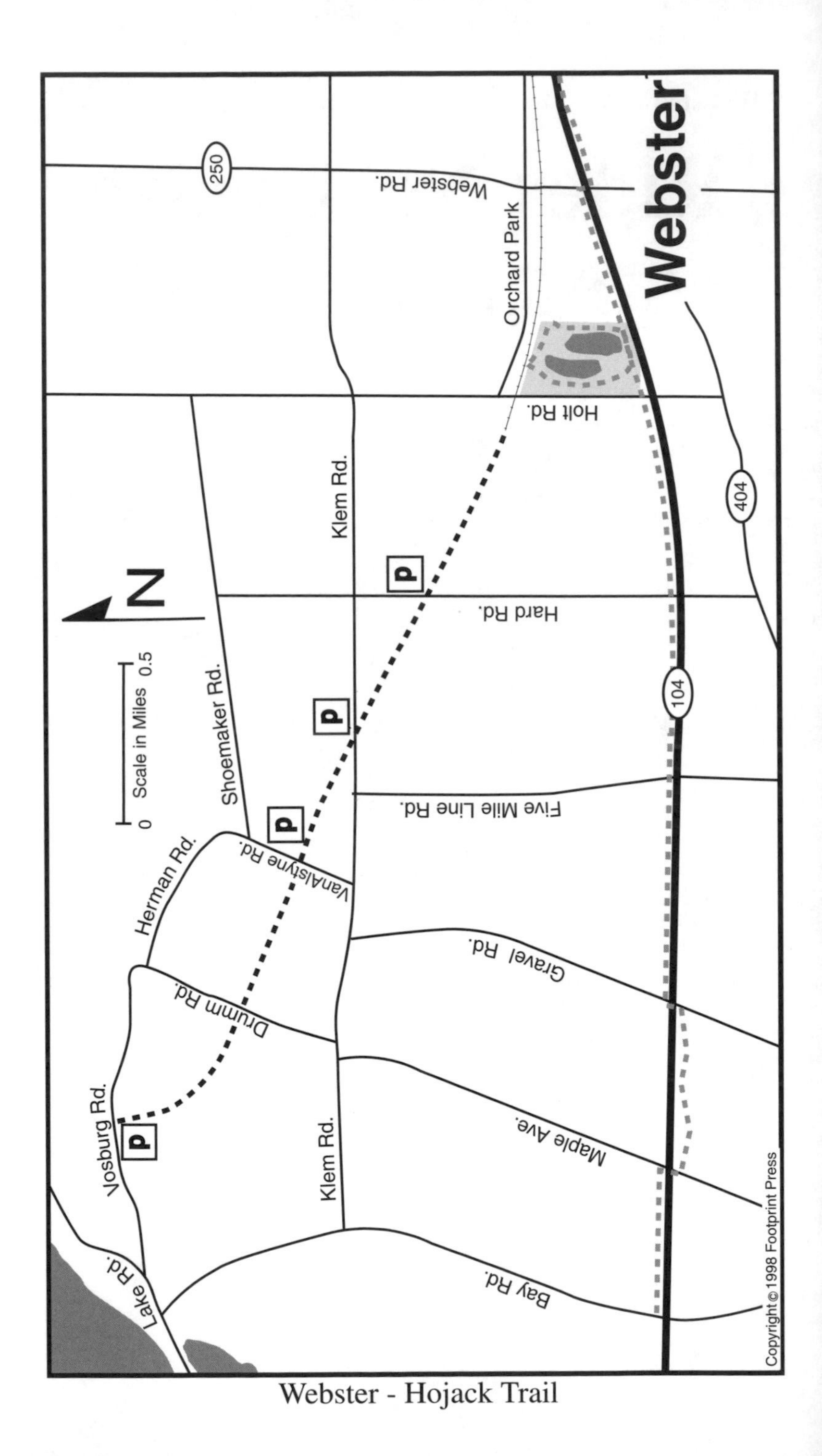

Webster - Hojack Trail

5.

Webster - Hojack Trail

Location: Between Vosburg Road and North Ponds Park, Webster

Parking: Best access is from the southern end of Klem Road South School parking lot. Klem Road School is located just west of Holt Road.

Alternative Parking: At any of the road intersections. Vosburg, VanAlstyne, Klem, and Hard Roads all have space for several vehicles immediately adjacent to the Hojack Trail. There is a gravel parking lot on the north side of North Ponds Park, along Orchard Road; but trail access can be difficult because of the rails that run for several hundred yards west of Holt Road.

Riding Time: 30 minutes one way

Length: 3.5 miles one way

Difficulty: Moderate, level but bumpy

Surface: Grass and cinder path over an old gravel rail bed. The trail is maintained by volunteers to a minimum width of eight feet.

Trail Markings: None as of this writing; but they are in-progress

Uses:

Contact: Friends of Webster Trails
C/O Jack Kerson
1021 Gravel Road

Webster, NY 14580
(716) 671-0258

Friends of Webster Trails
C/O Webster Parks and Recreation Department
985 Ebner Drive
Webster, NY 14580
(716) 872-7103

This trail is a work in process. The old rail bed has been cleared of rails and ties for 3.5 miles but falls just short of connecting through to Holt Road and North Ponds Park. When this last section is cleared, it will make a great connection to the trails around North Ponds Park and the Webster-Route 104 Trail. Until then, you have to bike out and back or walk your bike less than ¼ mile over the rails to reach Holt Road. The Friends of Webster Trails plan to build hiking and biking trails in the five-acre wildlife area which is adjacent to the Hojack Trail near Vosburg Road.

Road crossings are currently marked with green-and-white signs that say "Private property - use by motorized vehicles, snowmobiles, and horseback riding is not authorized. Violators will be prosecuted. Rochester Gas and Electric Corp."

In the 1850s the farmers of Webster had three options for shipping their produce to market. They could endure an all-day wagon ride to Rochester, an eight-mile wagon ride to the Erie Canal in Fairport, or meet a schooner at Nine Mile Point on Lake Ontario. All were arduous choices.

The prominent businessmen of Webster worked with representatives from other towns between Lewiston and Oswego to inspire the creation of the Lake Ontario Shore Railroad Company in 1868. In 1876 trains began arriving and departing from the Webster station. The line was sold to the Rome, Watertown and Ogdensburg Railroad and the abbreviations R.W. & O.R.R. became known as "Rotten Wood and Old Rusty Rails."

In 1889 a major crash occurred as a westbound train from the Thousand Islands rammed a train as it boarded passengers bound to Rochester. Many Webster homes became temporary hospitals to care for the injured. This crash brought about the use of automotive brakes on railroads.

The Webster train station became a hub of activity. In the fall, the railroad was hard pressed to supply enough cars to transport all of the apples from local orchards. The Basket Factory was built along the tracks and became the largest and most productive basket factory in the world. Companies such as the Webster Canning and Preserving Company (a predecessor to Curtice-Burns), the Basket

Rich near the metal yellow barrier at Drumm Road.

Factory, John W. Hallauer and Sons Evaporated Fruits, Martin Brothers Lumber Company, Webster Lumber Company, and LeFrois Pickling Factory, all owed their existence to the railroad.

This rail line, like all others in the area, was doomed by the increase in trucks and automobiles. Thanks to the Friends of Webster Trails it became a hiking and biking trail in 1997. To read more about the history of this rail line and the Hojack Station, check their web site at www.frontiernet.net/~dbaird/friends.htm.

Trail Directions

•From the parking lot of the Klem Road South School, walk south, across the ball diamonds, and you will find easy access to the trail. (The trail to the left (E) is not yet cleared to Holt Road.)
•Turn right (W) along the 8-foot-wide rail bed.
•On your right, watch for the cement pillar with a "W," telling the train conductor to blow the whistle.
•Cross Hard Road.
•At Klem Road, cross diagonally toward the right.
•Cross VanAlstyne Road.
•Pass an old cement railroad post inscribed "P87," denoting 87 miles to Pulaski. Pulaski must have been a major port into Lake Ontario in the heyday of the railroads.
•Pass a yellow metal trail barricade and cross Drumm Road
•At Vosburg Road, turn around and retrace the path.

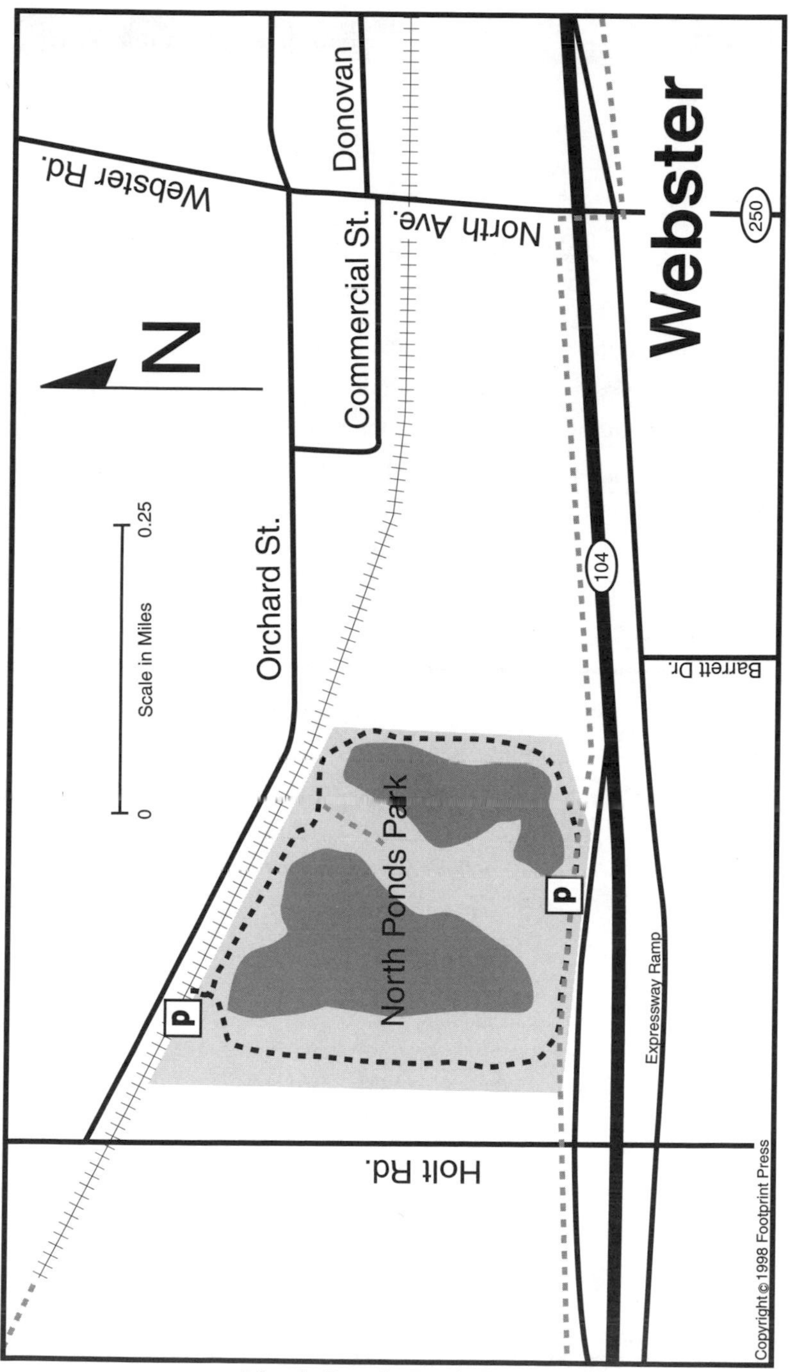

North Ponds Park Trail

6.

North Ponds Park Trail

Location: North Ponds Park, Webster (between Route 104 and Orchard Road)

Parking: Free lot on Orchard Road.

Alternative Parking: Off westbound Route 104 entrance ramp off North Avenue - pay in summer (June 13 through August 31), free in winter.

Riding Time: 15 minutes

Length: 1.3 mile loop

Difficulty: Easy, level

Surface: Gravel path and paved path

Trail Markings: None

Uses:

Contact: Webster Parks and Recreation Department
985 Ebner Drive
Webster, NY 14580
(716) 872-2911

North Ponds Park has a popular swimming area in summer. A level trail circumnavigates the park's two largest ponds and makes a nice ride at any time of the year (unless it's covered in snow). The area can be somewhat noisy from traffic on nearby Route 104.

Trail Directions

•From the parking lot on Orchard Road, follow the path into the park.

•At the "Y" junction bear right.

•Follow the path, bearing left as it winds around the ponds, past the restrooms, swimming area, snack bar, etc.

•Bear right at the "Y" junction. (Left path leads between the two ponds to a picnic area.)

•Turn right at the next junction to return to the parking lot.

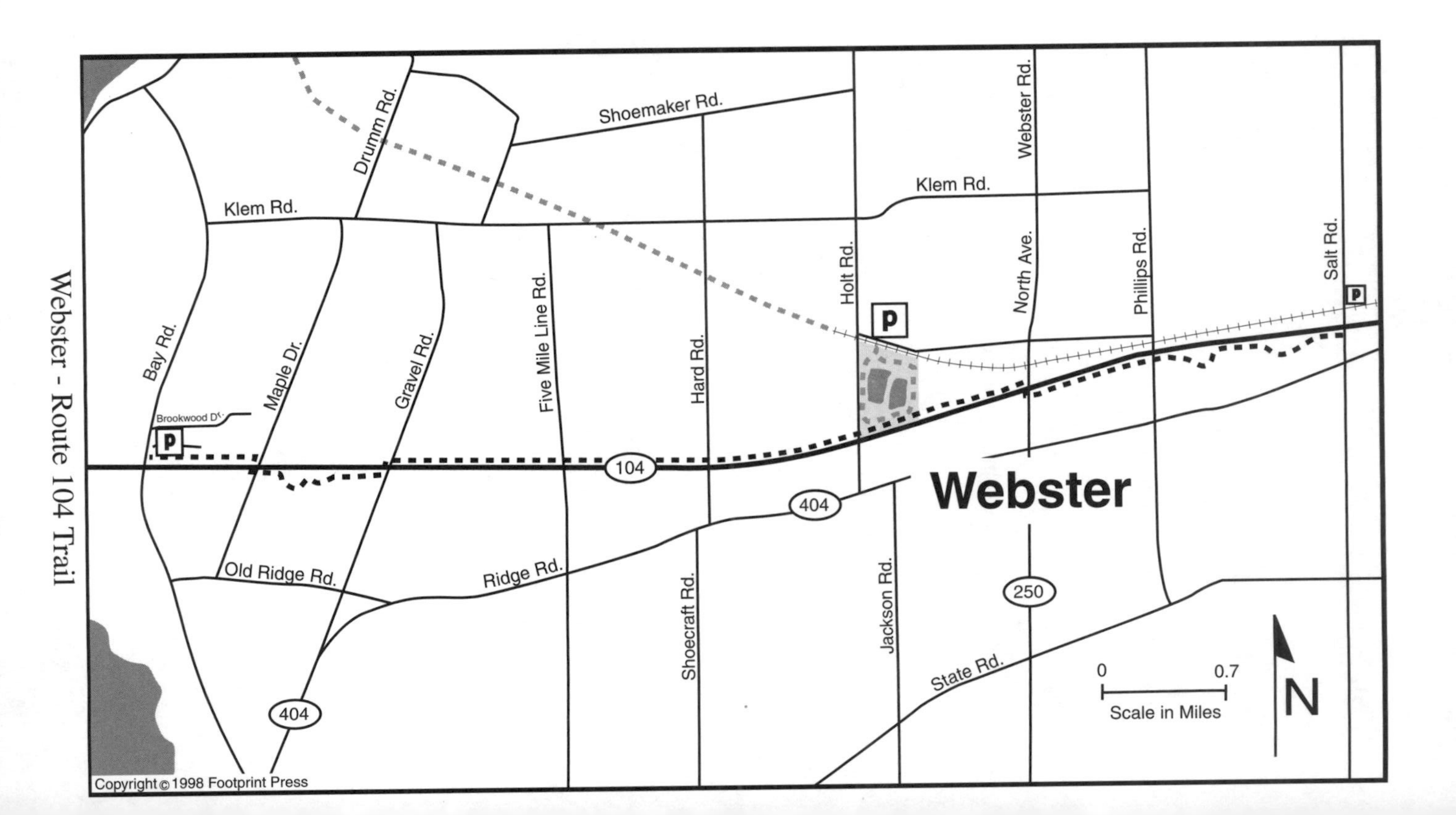

Webster - Route 104 Trail

7.

Webster - Route 104 Trail

Location: Bay Road to Salt Road, Webster

Parking: Near the corner of Bay Road and Route 104 (From Bay Road take a right onto Brookwood Drive. Turn right onto Bayside Drive and follow it around to the right. Park in the cul-de-sac at the end of the road.)

Alternative Parking: North Ponds Park parking lots, north of Route 104 on Orchard Road

New York State Department of Transportation parking lot on Salt Road just north of Route 104

Riding Time: 1 hour one way

Length: 6.1 miles one way

Difficulty: Easy, gentle hills

Surface: Paved (asphalt)

Trail Markings: Green-and-white metal signs on posts showing a bicycle and the words “Bike Route”

Uses:

Contact: Town of Webster, Town Hall
1000 Ridge Road
Webster, NY 14580
(716) 872-1000

This paved path was completed in the fall of 1997 and it makes a great 12-mile journey out and back. Or, connect this trail with the North Ponds Park or Webster - Hojack Trails to make your own adventure. Although this trail parallels Route 104, sometimes on the north side, and sometimes on the south side, it is a separate bike path that stays a safe distance from the busy highway. Be sure to use crosswalks when crossing roads and obey all traffic signals.

Distances between main roads:

Bay Road to Maple Drive	0.9 mile
Maple Drive to Gravel Road	0.4 mile
Gravel Road to Five Mile Line Road	0.9 mile
Five Mile Line Road to Hard Road	0.7 mile
Hard Road to Holt Road	0.7 mile
Holt Road to Route 250	0.9 mile
Route 250 to Phillips Road	0.7 mile
Phillips Road to Salt Road	0.9 mile

Trail Directions

•From the cul-de-sac parking lot near the corners of Bay Road and Route 104, head around the guard rails, ride over the grass toward Route 104 and turn left (E) on the paved path.

•At Maple Drive turn right and ride under Route 104. Immediately after the bridge, cross Maple Drive and continue on the bike path south of Route 104.

•Pass several retention ponds.

•At Gravel Road, cross under Route 104 again, cross Gravel Road, and continue on the bike path north of Route 104.

•Cross Five Mile Line Road using the crosswalk and traffic light.

•Cross Hard Road. You've come 2.9 miles.

•Cross Holt Road.

•Pass through the southern edge of North Ponds Park. You can extend your ride with a loop around the ponds, stop for a swim, have a snack at the snack bar, or visit the restrooms.

•At Route 250 (South Avenue) turn right under the Route 104 bridge. Then cross Route 250 and continue on the bike path.

(Side Trip: North on Route 250, you'll find a Bagel Bin Café, Martino's Pizzeria, and Hank's Ice Cream Shop.)

•Cross Phillips Road. You've come 5.2 miles.

•Pass the Holy Trinity Church cemetery and a holding pond. The path winds through the woods until it meets Salt Road.

•At Salt Road the trail ends (6.1 miles). You can turn around and head back or take a left under the bridge to find the New York State Department of Transportation parking lot just north of Route 104.

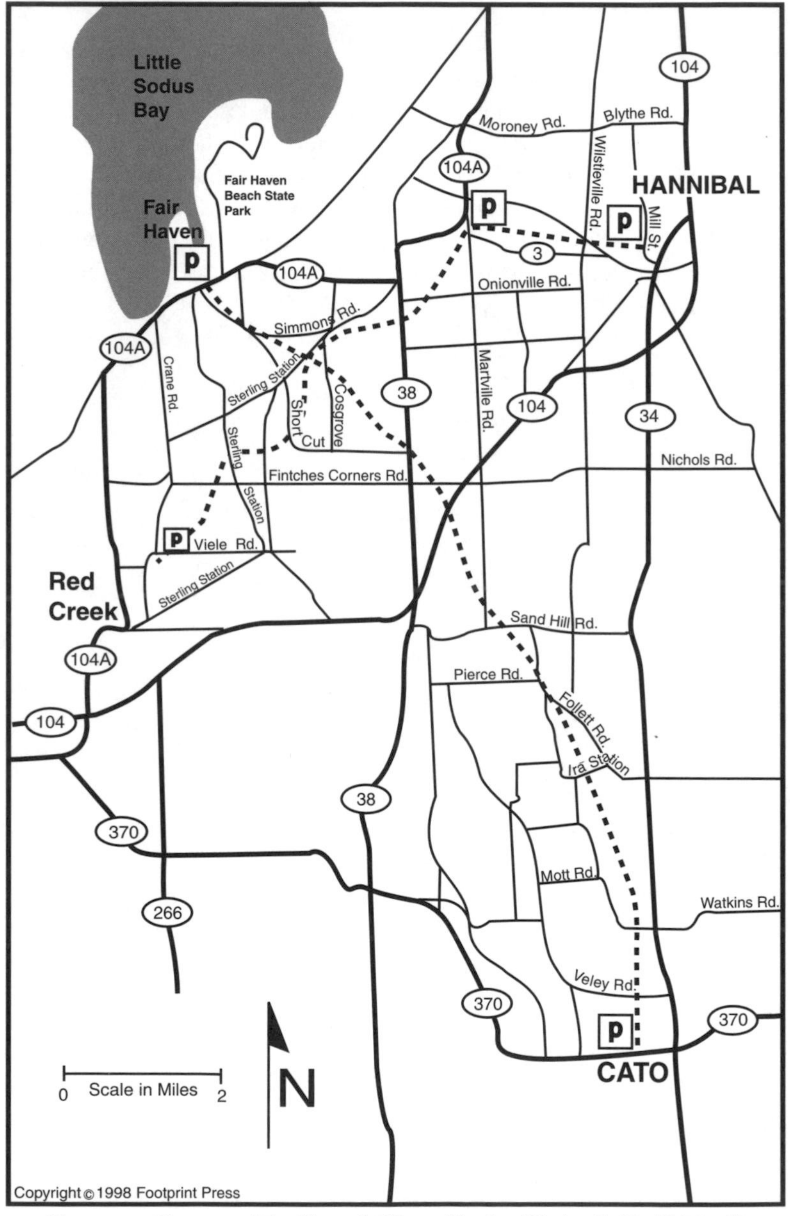

Cayuga County Trail and Hannibal - Hojack Rail Trail

8.

Cayuga County Trail

Location:	Fair Haven to Cato
Parking:	Southeast side of Route 104A, Fair Haven (a dirt parking area at a brown-and-yellow sign saying "Cayuga County Trail." Located between NY Pizzeria and St. Jude Chapel. Across the street is Hadcock Sales and Guiseppe's Sub and Pizza Shop.)
Alternative Parking:	Route 370, west of Cato
Riding Time:	1.5 hours one way
Length:	13 miles one way
Difficulty:	Easy, mostly level
Surface:	Cinder and mowed grass
Trail Markings:	Brown signs with yellow lettering "Cayuga County Trail, Fair Haven - Cato, 14 miles" Road crossings have stop signs
Uses:	
Contact:	Tom Higgins, County Planner Cayuga County Planning Board 160 Genesee Street Auburn, NY 13021-1276 (315) 253-1276

Meg Rogers
Cayuga County Office of Tourism
131 Genesee Street
Auburn, NY 13021
(800) 499-9615

Here's a pleasant country ride to get you away from urban chaos. The trail is mainly a raised bed through woods, swamps, and Christmas tree farms. It's an easy ride, shaded by a canopy of trees. In wet weather, be ready to ride through and around some puddles. The trail starts in Fair Haven, home of the 865-acre, Fair Haven Beach State Park, which has cabins and camping. Consider making this trail a weekend getaway, camping at the park and biking during the day. If it's warm, bring your swimsuits for a dip in Lake Ontario at the park's beach. Enjoy a meal at the Pleasant Beach Hotel and Restaurant overlooking Little Sodus Bay, or savor the homemade pastries at the Fly By Night Cookie Company.

Cato is nestled among the unique glacial ridges known as drumlins. The Cato Hotel and Tavern on Route 370 is located just one block east of the trail.

Like other rail trails in this book (#15, 16, 17, and 20), this section was part of the Lehigh Valley Railroad, which transported coal and farm products from Pennsylvania to Lake Ontario where the cargo was transferred to steamships.

Lodging: Black Creek Farm B&B, Mixer Road, Fair Haven, (315) 947-5282
Brown's Village Inn, Stafford Street, Fair Haven, (315) 947-5817
Frost Haven Resort, West Bay Road, Fair Haven, (315) 947-5331

Tours: Renaissance Festival is a short ride to the east in Sterling, NY, offering fun for the whole family weekends during the summer, (800) 879-4446.

A wetland along the Cayuga CountyTrail.

Distances between major roads:

Fair Haven to Sterling Station Road	1.6 miles
Sterling Station Road to Route 38	2.0 miles
Route 38 to Fintches Corners Road	0.7 mile
Fintches Corners Road to Route 104	0.3 mile
Route 104 to Sand Hill Road	2.0 miles
Sand Hill Road to Follett Road	1.2 miles
Follett Road to Ira Station Road	1.1 miles
Ira Station Road to Watkins Road	2.2 miles
Watkins Road to Route 370	1.7 miles

Trail Directions

- From the Fair Haven parking lot, head southeast along the trail.
- Cross Simmons Road.
- Cross Sterling Station Road and continue straight. The Hannibal Trail (trail #9, 7.4 miles long) crosses here. This was part of the Hojack Rail System.
- Pass a tall metal post on your left just before Cosgrove Road. It was a low-bridge indicator for crew members standing on top of the trains. When the railroad was active, trains passed under Cosgrove Road.
- Head uphill and cross Cosgrove Road.
- Pass numerous farm lanes and notice the Christmas tree farms along the way.
- Cross Route 38.
- Cross Fintches Corners Road. You've come 4.3 miles.
- The trail turns to mowed grass between Fintches Corners Road and Route 104. An old warehouse is on your right. The path parallels Queens Farms Road.
- Cross Route 104. Ride on a metal bridge over Sterling Creek. If you see signs saying "No Wheeled Vehicles," you can ignore them. They mean ATVs. Bicycles are allowed on this trail.
- Pass ponds on your left. This is a scenic spot to take a break.
- Cross Martville Road.
- Cross Sand Hill Road.

•Head downhill to cross a small creek. If you're lucky, cows will be grazing along the creek to your left.
•Cross Pierce Road. You've come 7.5 miles.
•Ride across a small bridge over a creek.
•Cross Follett Road. This is a short, rough section. A pond on the right is partly hidden by a line of trees along the trail.
•Cross Ira Station Road. To the right is Ira Corners, which was settled in 1805. By 1820 this town had two stores and a hotel.
•Continue past a beautiful pond/wetland on your right.
•Cross Watkins Road. You've come 11.1 miles.
•Cross Veley Road.
•The trail ends at Route 370. To your right is the first gristmill in Ira Corners, built in 1818 by John Hooker. The town of Cato is uphill to the left. It has a hardware store, grocery store, diner, pizza restaurant, gas station, and the Cato Hotel and Tavern.

9.

Hannibal - Hojack Rail Trail

Location: Red Creek to Hannibal (see map on page 68)

Parking: North side on Viele Road (Follow Route 104A north through Red Creek. In the village, pass Viele's Agway and turn right at the Red Creek Fire Department. Turn left at the first intersection onto Viele Road. Park at the trail intersection.)

Alternative Parking: Martville Road
Mill Street

Riding Time: 1.25 hours one way

Length: 7.4 miles one way

Difficulty: Easy, mostly level

Surface: Gravel path

Trail Markings: None

Uses:

Contact: Tom Higgins, County Planner
Cayuga County Planning Board
160 Genesee Street
Auburn, NY 13021-1276
(315) 253-1276

Meg Rogers
Cayuga County Office of Tourism

131 Genesee Street
Auburn, NY 13021
(800) 499-9615

This trail was part of the Hojack Rail System, just like the Webster Section (trail #5). The area is rugged, and the trail winds around the hills and follows the creeks and streams, making it a more enjoyable ride than one that goes in a straight line to its destination. Work is proceeding to extend the rail trail from Viele Road through Red Creek and into Monroe County.

Lodging: Maplegrove B&B, State Route 104A, Sterling, NY, (315) 947-5408
Also see listings under trail #8

Tours: Renaissance Festival is a short ride to the east in Sterling, NY, offering fun for the whole family weekends during the summer, (800) 879-4446.

A shed and play tire along the Hannibal - Hojack Rail Trail.

Distances between major roads:

Viele Road to Sterling Station Road	2.0 miles
Sterling Station Road to Route 38	1.6 miles
Route 38 to Martville Road	1.6 miles
Martville Road to Mill Street	2.2 miles

Trail Directions

•After parking along Viele Road, head NE. (Note: The trail going SE comes to a dead end within 0.5 mile.)
•Cross Fintches Corners Road.
•Cross a bridge.
•Dip down as you cross Sterling Station Road.
•Cross Humphrey Road.
•Cross Short Cut Road.
•Cross Cayuga County Trail (trail #8). You are now riding parallel to Sterling Station Road.
•Cross Cosgrove Road. The trail veers east, away from Sterling Station Road.
•Cross a bridge.
•Cross Route 38.
•Cross another bridge.
•Cross Onionville Road.
•Cross Martville Road. Parking is available here.
•Cross another bridge.
•Cross Wilstieville Road.
•A creek passes under the trail through a culvert.
•The trail ends at Mill Street. Parking is available here. The village of Hannibal is 0.5 mile away. It has a gas station, pizza shop, and ice cream shop. To reach Hannibal, turn right (S) onto Mill Street, then take a right onto Oswego Street.

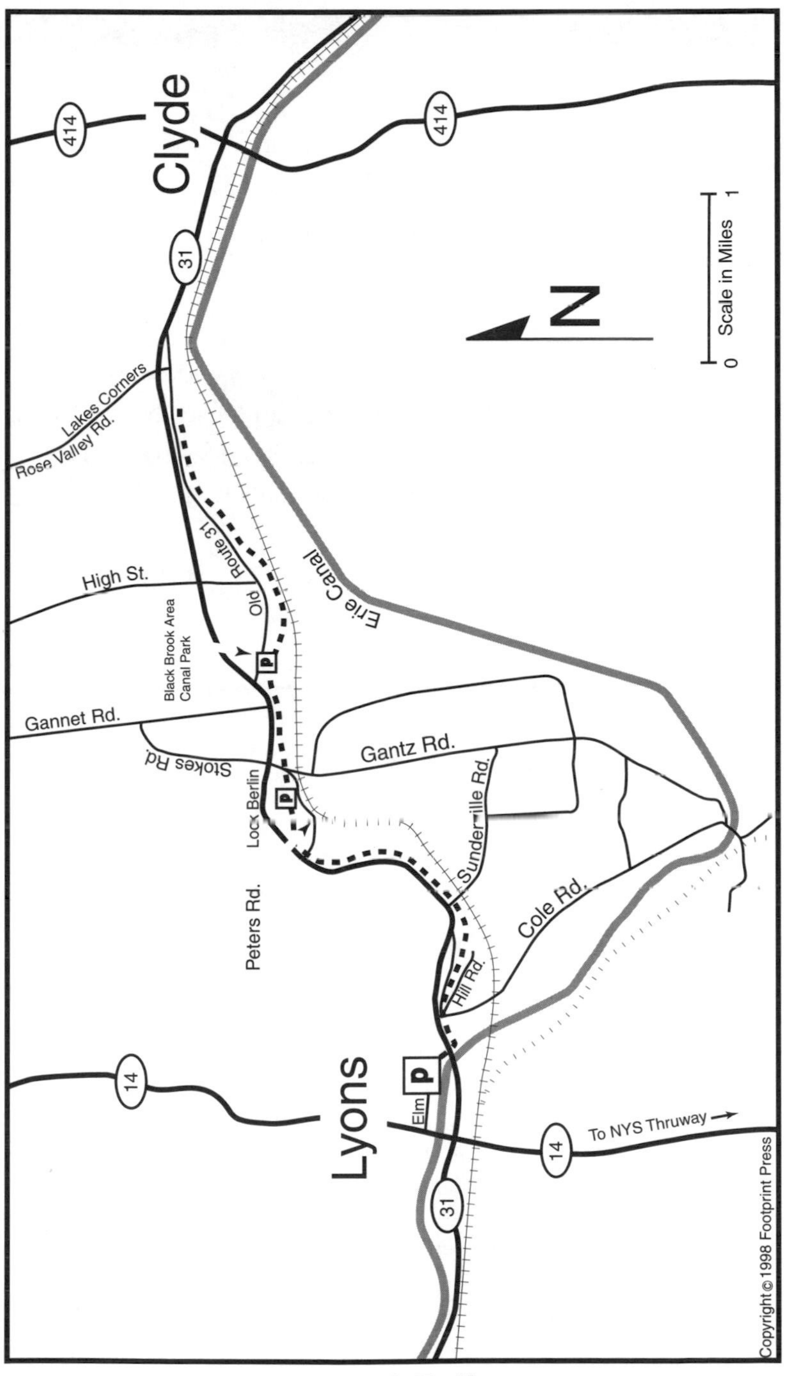

Canal Park Trailway

10.

Canal Park Trailway

Location:	Lyons to Clyde
Parking:	Village of Lyon's Public Works Department (Head north on Route 14, over the Erie Canal. Turn right onto Elm Street. Drive until the road ends, past the Little League Field.)
Alternative Parking:	At road crossings The intersection of Route 31 and Old Route 31
Riding Time:	1 hour one way
Length:	5.8 miles one way
Difficulty:	Moderate, some hills, soft path
Surface:	Mowed-grass path
Trail Markings:	2 by 3-foot, white, blue, and red signs
Uses:	
Contact:	Wayne County Planning Department Jim Coulombe 9 Pearl Street Lyons, NY 14489 (315) 946-5919

Follow history back in time as you pedal from the existing Erie Canal to the original Clinton's Ditch of 1817 and the enlarged Erie Canal of the 1850s. Along the way pass stone locks long abandoned. On one trip we saw wild turkey and a beaver repairing his den. Locals say the old canal waters are a great fishing spot for bass and sunfish.

The Erie Canal, dubiously called "Clinton's Ditch," opened for operation in 1825. It was a 40-foot-wide water channel with locks 90 feet long and 15 feet wide. Boats with loads up to 75 tons could navigate the waters. By 1840 a greater capacity was needed as commerce along the canal boomed, and the canal was enlarged to 70 feet wide. Locks increased to 110 feet long and 18 feet wide allowing cargos up to 200 tons.

By 1909, the canal was overcapacity again. This time the canal was rerouted in places as it was enlarged. The name was changed to reflect its growing purpose. The new-and-improved Barge Canal opened in 1918 allowing cargos of 3,000 tons to pass through its 45-foot-wide locks. The opening of the Saint Lawrence Seaway eliminated the need to transfer goods to barges and rendered the the canal obsolete. The name was changed back to its historic one: the Erie Canal.

You can zip to and from this adventure on the New York State Thruway, but why not slow down and follow Route 96 for at least one leg of the journey. You'll be rewarded with tours through stately old towns and spectacular examples of cobblestone houses along the way.

Distances between major roads:

Route 14 to Hill Road	0.7 mile
Hill Road to Sunderville Road	0.7 mile
Sunderville Road to Peters Road	1.0 mile
Peters Road to Gansz Road	0.6 mile
Gansz Road to Black Brook Area Canal Park	0.7 mile
Black Brook Area Canal Park to Route 31	2.1 miles

Trail Directions

•From the sign saying "Canal Park Trailway" at the end of Elm Street, Lyons, head east through the backyard of a grey, boarded-up apartment complex. The current Erie Canal is to your right.

- Ride under the Route 31 bridge. Beware of a small washout under the bridge.
- The trail winds left, away from the canal to parallel Route 31.
- Stay on the grass path. It leads over a pedestrian bridge to cross a small creek.
- Continue uphill parallel to Route 31.
- Ride across Cross Road.
- Ride on Old Route 31 road for a short distance.
- At the intersection of Hill Road, continue straight on the grass path between Old Route 31 and Hill Road.
- Pass an old stone bridge abutment. Clinton's Ditch is on your left.
- Cross Sunderville Road. Clinton's Ditch continues to be on your left.
- Cross Peter's Road.
- Pass an abandoned, stone, double lock. A park is at the lock (Berlin Lock) with picnic tables and grills.
- Cross Gansz Road. The canal is dammed here and becomes a trickle in a ditch from here east.
- Cross a small wooden bridge.
- A short side trail to the left goes to stonework around a feeder creek, which is actually half of an original Clinton's Ditch lock rebuilt to form a waste weir.
- A path to the left, across a crooked wooden bridge, leads to Black Brook Area Canal Park. This park has restrooms, a pavilion, picnic tables, grills, and a playground.
- The mowed path ends at a driveway. You can turn around here to head back or turn left onto the driveway, then right (E) onto Old Route 31, and ride 0.9 mile to the junction of Route 31 where parking is available.

Rides Southeast of Rochester

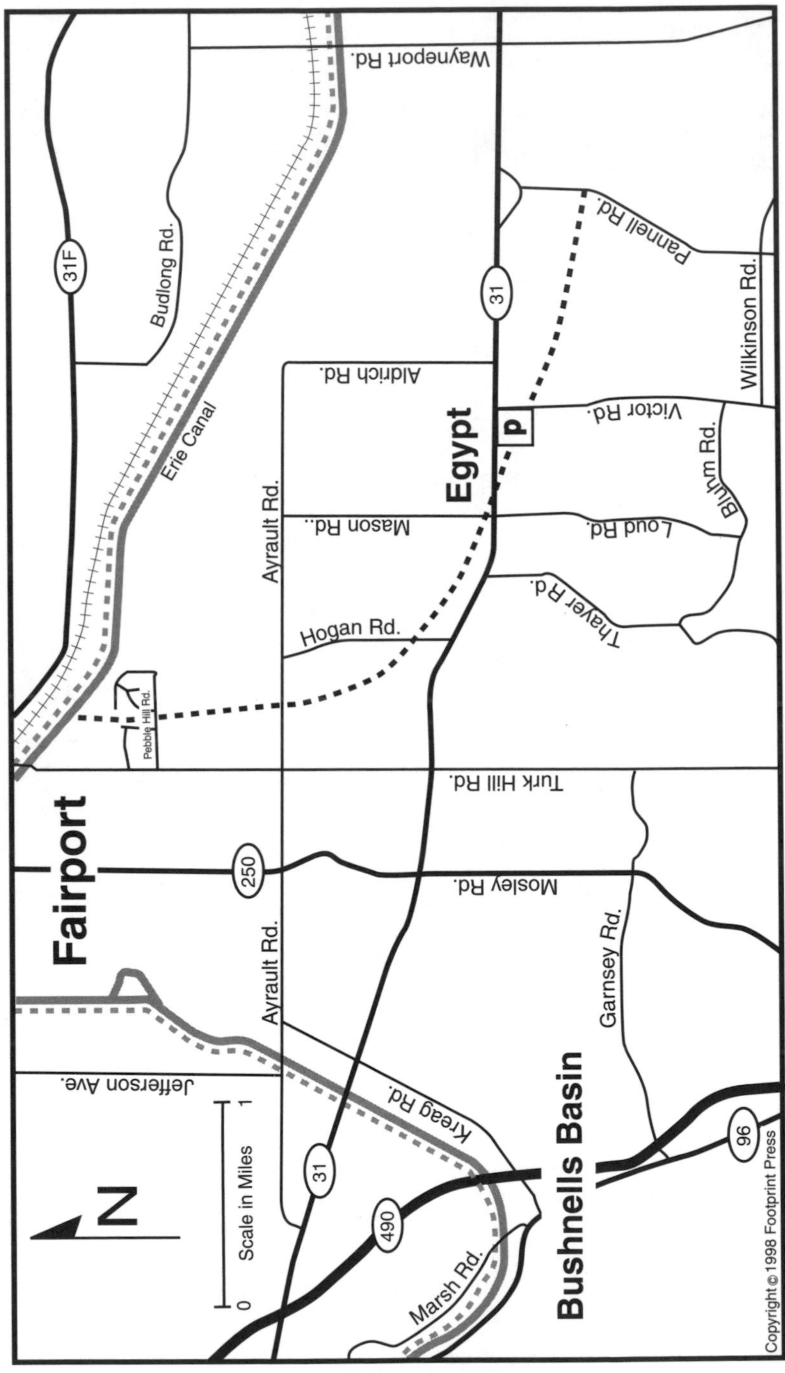

Perinton Hikeway/Bikeway

11.

Perinton Hikeway/Bikeway

Location: Erie Canal to Pannell Road, Perinton
Parking: Egypt Park on Victor Road, near the corner of Pittsford-Palmyra Road (Route 31)
Alternative Parking: None
Riding Time: 35 minutes one way
Length: 4.4 miles one way
Difficulty: Easy, level
Surface: Ground, packed stone, and some mowed grass
Trail Markings: Green-and-white signs at road intersections:
"No Motorized Vehicles on Bike-Hikeway"
"Rochester, Syracuse, & Eastern Trolley Trail"
Uses:
Contact: Town of Perinton
Recreation and Parks Department
1350 Turk Hill Road
Fairport, NY 14450
(716) 223-5050

The path you will ride once carried two electric trolley lines operated by the Rochester, Syracuse, and Eastern Rapid Railroad from 1906 until 1931. It was part of the Beebe Syndicate, a group of 12 high-speed, interurban, electric train lines which ran from Buffalo, through Rochester and Syracuse, then north to Oswego. The Rochester, Syracuse & Eastern Rapid Railroad portion ran from downtown Rochester to Auburn through East Rochester, Fairport, Egypt, Palmyra, Newark, and others. A car house was located between Port Gibson and Newark.

In 1908 the fare from Fairport to Rochester was $.15 one way and $.25 round trip. People of the time complained about the excessive fees. The RS&E cost $144,000 per mile to build (far more than an average railroad) and never made a profit in its short 25-year history. There were three reasons for its failure to prosper. First, it competed with an existing steam railroad and was never able to garner enough of the lucrative freight business. Second, its initial cost was too great for its earning capacity. And, finally, like all interurbans, it lost out to the competition of the gasoline engine, as cars became the transportation mode of choice.

East Rochester was changed by the RS&E. Originally established as the town of Despatch in 1893, the townsfolk voted to change their name after the trolley came to town. A substation in the village still bears the Despatch name and is used today by Xerox Corporation.

Today the Perinton Hikeway/Bikeway traverses suburban backyards and remote woods. Before or after your ride, enjoy the restrooms, tennis courts, picnic tables, and swing sets in Egypt Park. A must for any visit is a walk around the animal pens of Lollypop Farm to see horses, ponies, donkeys, llamas, English fallow deer, geese, ducks, goats, and sheep. For a donation of $1.00 you can enter the petting area with llamas and goats. The animal shelter building houses dogs and cats looking for new homes.

English fallow deer at Lollypop Farm.

Perinton Hikeway/Bikeway

There is no parking at either end of this trail. The route described leaves from Egypt Park, heads northwest to the Erie Canal. It then reverses, goes past the start point, and heads toward the eastern end at Pannell Road. Once again it reverses and returns to the start at Egypt Park. So, a round trip (8.8 miles) is achieved from a parking spot midway between the ends of the trail.

Trail Directions

•From the parking lot at Egypt Park, head to the path at the far corner (SW).
•Follow this path over a wooden bridge.
•Turn right (W) on the grassy bike path. Straight ahead is the way to Lollypop Farm.
•Cross Pittsford-Palmyra Road (Route 31).
•Cross through the front of the parking lot at the Egypt Fire Department.
•Cross Mason Road and continue on the eight-foot-wide, crushed stone bikeway.
•Cross Hogan Road.
•Cross Ayrault Road. In 1812 Egypt's first tavern and stage-coach stop was built along here. The building was moved in 1985 and is now the Oliver Loud Country Inn on the canal in Bushnell's Basin.
•Cross Pebble Hill Road. The path turns back to mowed grass and dirt.
•The path ends at the Erie Canal and the intersection with an orange-blazed Crescent Trail. Do not bike on the orange trail.
•After enjoying the canal, turn around and retrace your path.
•Continue past the Egypt Park and Lollypop Farm side trails.
•Cross Victor Road. The path is crushed stone once again.
•Pass through a swamp area filled with cattails and the trunks of many dead trees.
•The western end of the trail arrives at the yellow posts before Pannell Road.
•Turn around and retrace your path back to Egypt Park.

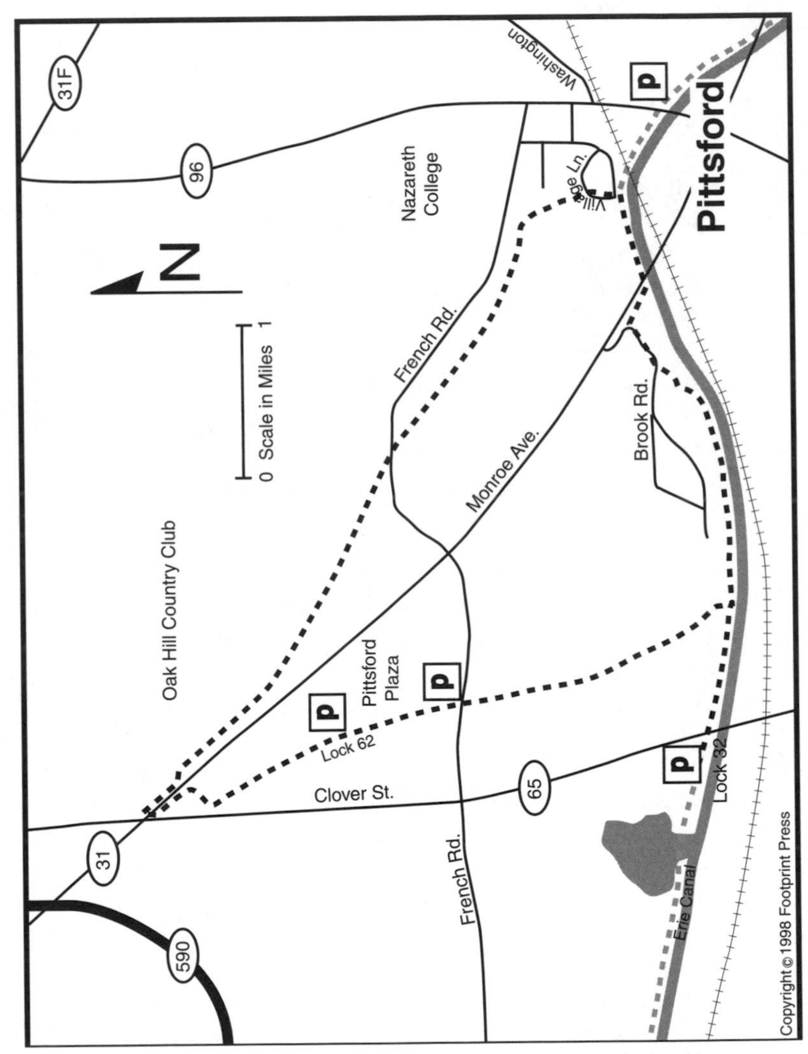

Historic Erie Canal and Railroad Loop Trail

12.

Historic Erie Canal and Railroad Loop Trail

Location: Lock 32 Canal Park, Pittsford (Clover Street / Route 65)

Parking: Lock 32 Canal Park parking area, Clover Street / Route 65

Alternative Parking: French Road, near Clover Street
Lock 62 Canal Park in Wegman's parking lot at Pittsford Plaza

Riding Time: 50 minutes

Length: 6-mile loop

Difficulty: Easy, mostly level, some hills

Surface: Mowed grass path, paved path

Trail Markings: None

Uses:

Contact: Pittsford Parks Department
35 Lincoln Avenue
Pittsford, NY 14534
(716) 248-6280

As the name of the trail implies, you will be biking on not one, but two historic paths of transportation. The original Erie Canal, known as "Clinton's Ditch," headed north to Rochester. It was opened in 1822, enlarged in the 1850s, and closed in 1919. Mules and horses pulled the canal boats on a towpath next to the canal. You'll bike on some of it. The rest is now Interstates 390 and 490. Along the way, you'll see evidence of the Odenbach Shipyard, which made landing craft during World War II, and Lock 62 built in 1855 as part of the first canal expansion and abandoned in 1918 when the new canal was routed south of Rochester.

Abandoned double Lock 62.

You'll pass the Spring House Restaurant, a lovely federal-style building built in 1829 or 1830 as an Erie Canal inn. At its peak, this area included a resort and spa with a healing sulphur and mineral spring, an amusement pavillion, and bowling alleys.

Then it's on to the Rochester and Auburn rail bed, an active railroad from 1840 through 1960. It was the first railroad east of Rochester and became part of the New York Central system. Both of these sections are maintained by the Pittsford Parks Department and the Pittsford Trails Coalition.

The third leg of the trip takes you along the present-day Erie Canal for a scenic ride back to Lock 32 Canal Park. Lock 32 was built in 1912 and still operates today.

Bike Shop: Park Avenue Bike Shop, 2920 Monroe Avenue, (716) 381-3080

Trail Directions

- Begin by heading east on the paved canal towpath. Walk your bike down a flight of stairs. Cross underneath Route 65, where you have a great view of the bottom of a lock.
- After 0.4 mile the path heads slightly inland from the canal. Make a sharp left turn (N) off the paved path onto a mowed-grass path at the map post showing the "Historic Erie Canal & Railroad Loop Trail."
- As you're riding on the 20-foot-wide grass path, notice the remains of the old canal bed on your left.
- The path becomes an old asphalt road. Remains of the Odenbach Shipyard are on the left.
- Cross French Road and the trail parking area. The trail narrows to 6 feet.
- The rear of Pittsford Plaza emerges on your right.
- The access trail down to Wegman's parking is on the right.
- Dual Lock 62 is on your left.
- Follow the trail down steps and then over a small wooden bridge.
- Turn right after the bridge. (Trail to the left goes to homes.)
- Now you're riding on the old canal bed. Trail widens to 10 feet.
- Trail exits at the Spring House Restaurant parking lot.
- Head through the parking lot to the sidewalk along Monroe Avenue. Turn left and follow the sidewalk to the intersection of Clover Street.
- Cross Monroe Avenue. Be sure to use the crosswalk on this busy street.
- Turn right (E) onto Monroe Avenue along the sidewalk. The trail begins again between Clover Commons and the Park Avenue Bike Shop. This next segment of the trail is on the old Rochester and Auburn railbed.
- The trail passes behind many buildings on Monroe Avenue.

- There are some short, rough sections on ballast stone, and you also cross the rear parking lots of some stores.
- Cross French Road and continue along the railroad bed.
- A cement pillar with a "W" is on the left. It alerted the train conductor to blow his whistle.
- As you approach a red brick, commercial storage building, take the trail to the right (SE).
- Bear left at the "T" junction at a pine forest. Ride toward a red-brick building.
- Turn right on the paved road and follow it around to the canal towpath, keeping the round, red-brick building on your left.
- At the canal towpath, turn right (E).
- Ride under the Monroe Avenue bridge.
- Follow the canal-trail signs and turn right at the NYS Canal Maintenance property.
- Take a left onto Brook Road.
- Turn left at the yellow metal gate to complete the circle around the NYS Canal Maintenance property and return uphill to the towpath along the canal.
- Follow the canal towpath to Lock 32 Canal Park.

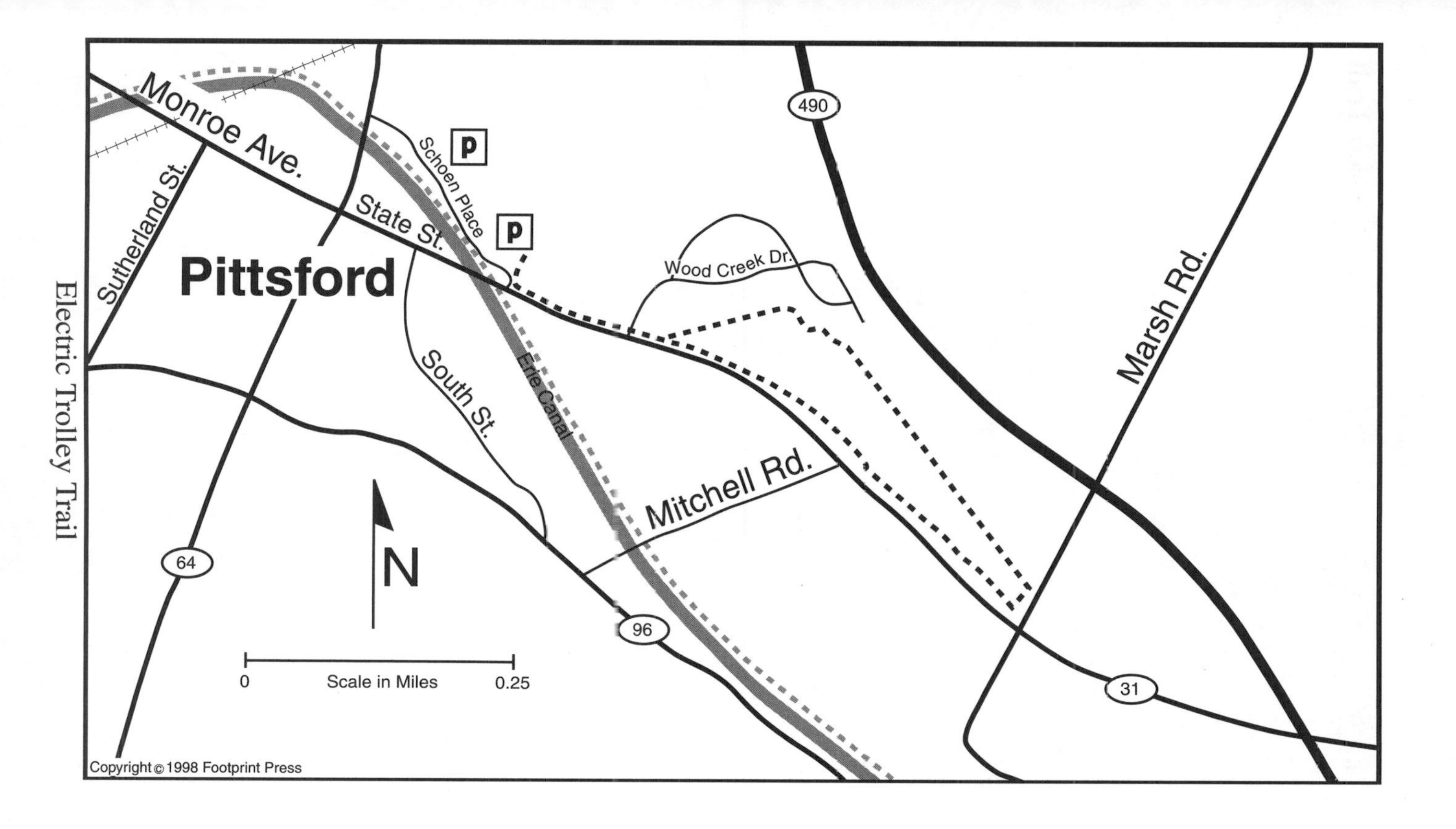

Electric Trolley Trail

13.

Electric Trolley Trail

Location:	Just east of the village of Pittsford, near Route 31
Parking:	Park in Northfield Commons, 50 State Street (at the east end of Schoen Place)
Alternative Parking:	Schoen Place parking lot, near the Coal Tower Restaurant
Riding Time:	20 minutes
Length:	1.8-mile loop
Difficulty:	Easy, rolling hills
Surface:	Half paved, half dirt path
Trail Markings:	None
Uses:	
Contact:	Pittsford Parks Department 35 Lincoln Avenue Pittsford, NY 14534 (71) 248-6280

This short loop begins in the village of Pittsford and follows rolling hills parallel to Route 31. At Marsh Road it turns into a dirt path and follows the previous route of the Rochester and Eastern Rapid Railway, which operated an electric trolley from 1903 until 1930. This was a popular route from Rochester to Geneva with 36 stops between the cities. Trees are labeled along the way with names like shag bark hickory, black oak, Norway maple, and black cherry. This trail can be connected with the Erie Canalway Trail (the towpath) to make a jaunt as long as you wish.

There are lots of shops and restaurants for you to enjoy in Northfield Commons and along Schoen Place.

Bike Shop: Towpath Bike Shop, 7 Schoen Place, (716) 381-2808

A sign along the Electric Trolley Trail, near Marsh Road.

Trail Directions

- From the Northfield Commons parking lot, ride east on the sidewalk along State Street, heading away from the Erie Canal. State Street turns into Pittsford-Palmyra Road (Route 31) as it leaves the village limits.
- Pass Wood Creek Drive. The paved bike path heads inland a bit so you're parallel to Route 31 behind a grove of trees. A farm field is on your left.
- Pass the entrance to the Highlands of Pittsford.
- The path bends left (N) as it nears Marsh Road.

- At a sign for the Rochester and Eastern Rapid Railway, the pavement ends. Turn left onto the old trolley bed. You are in a pleasant tunnel of trees.
- Twice you pass entrance roads to the Highlands of Pittsford as the trail becomes more hilly.
- The path winds left and crosses a field, parallel to power lines.
- Turn right when it intersects the paved path again, and follow the sidewalk back to Northfield Commons.

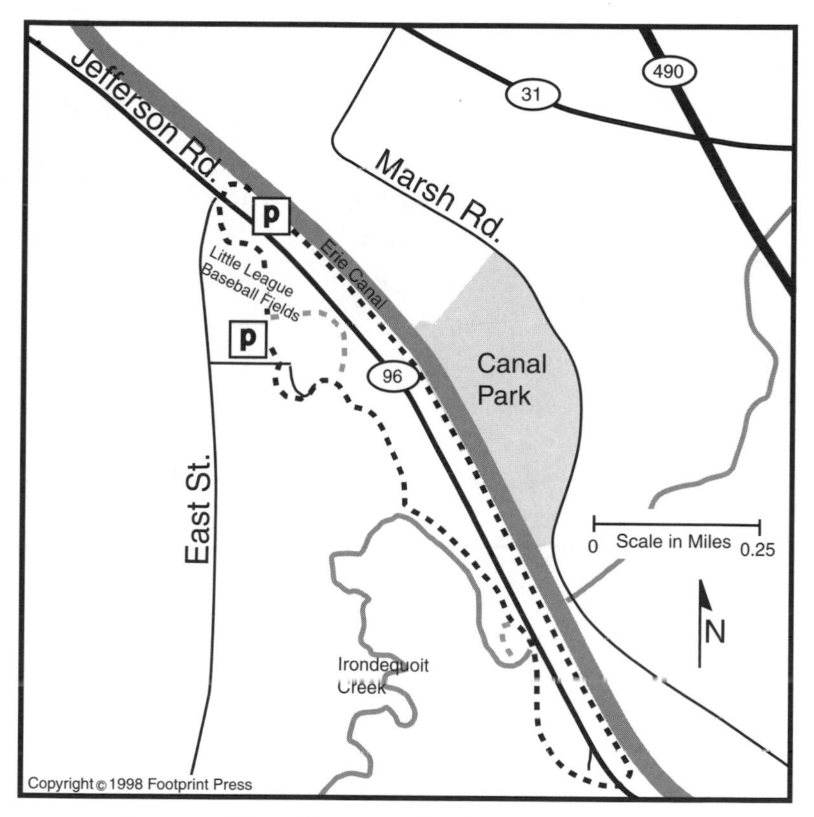

Cartersville - Great Embankment Loop Trail

14.

Cartersville - Great Embankment Loop Trail

Location: Along the Erie Canal and East Street, Pittsford
Parking: Little League parking lot on Robbins Road off East Street, near the corner of Jefferson Road (Route 96)
Alternative Parking: Route 96 near East Street next to the canal
Riding Time: 30 minutes
Length: 2.4-mile loop
Difficulty: Moderate, three short but steep hills
Surface: Mowed grass and dirt
Trail Markings: White and blue blazes, round metal "Pittsford Trails" logo
Uses:
Contact: Pittsford Parks Department
35 Lincoln Avenue
Pittsford, NY 14534
(716) 248-6280

The area you will ride is steeped in history. Once the site of Cartersville, a busy nineteenth century canal port, it had a distillery, warehouses, and a facility for changing the mules and horses that towed the canal boats.

You'll ride on top of the Great Embankment, one of the greatest achievements of the pioneer canal builders. Their challenge was to have the canal span the 70-foot-deep, one-mile-wide Irondequoit Creek Valley. They used earth from the local area to form mounds to join the natural glacial hills of the Pittsford esker. The great embankment was originally built in 1821-22 and was enlarged several times. It remains today, the highest canal embankment in the world.

Two guard gates, one just west of the trail and one at Bushnell's Basin, isolate this section of canal in case of leaks or breaks in the embankment, as happened in 1974 when contractor's tunneling under the embankment, inadvertently pierced the waterway. Forty homes were damaged or destroyed as the waters rushed downhill through a 100-foot hole in the bottom of the canal before the gates could be closed. As you cross the embankment, watch for manhole covers next to the canal. These provide access to ladders in a shaft leading to the creek 80 feet below, so that engineers can periodically check the embankment.

The section of Irondequoit Creek that you'll pass was once home to Simon Stone's gristmill and sawmill. Mr. Stone, a Revolutionary War veteran and founder of Pittsford, built his mills in the early 1790s. Milling in this area continued until 1913, when the canal enlargement displaced the mills

The trail follows close to the edge of the canal; watch small children carefully.

A break at the picnic table where Irondequoit Creek flows under Route 96 and the Erie Canal.

Trail Directions

•From the parking lot, head south over the grass toward the white blaze.

•Follow the blazes around the outside perimeter of a former dump, now grass covered.

•Cross over a culvert onto the dirt town-maintenance road.

•Bear right as the trail heads downhill, still following the white blazes. A blue-blazed trail enters from the left. It is a short cut-back to the ball fields.

•Follow the white-blazed path through the woods.

•Irondequoit Creek appears on the right. Jefferson Road (Route 96) is above you on the left.

•A path veers off to the right. For a short side venture, leave your bike and follow this path down some steps to Irondequoit Creek and a picnic table. The culvert you'll be looking at takes the creek under Route 96 and the canal. It was built in 1916.

•Back on the white-blazed trail, wind through the woods. Toward the top of a steep hill is a yellow metal barricade off Route 96, but bear right and continue uphill.

•When you reach Route 96, turn left and cross it, very carefully. The trail from here follows the south side of the canal very closely. If you have small children, you may want to walk the bikes. A right turn would connect into a Crescent Trail, but biking is not permitted.

•The towpath (Erie Canalway Trail) is on the opposite side of the canal.

•The canal along this section has high cement walls and banked sides. This is the highest point of the Great Embankment. Follow the mowed-grass path along the edge of the canal.

•Pass through a wooden rail fence and continue along the canal through a gravel parking and picnic area.

•Cross Route 96 when you reach East Street.

•Enter the woods immediately behind the East Street road sign.

•A blue trail heads off on the right. It's a very short loop to the Cartersville site, which you can take to extend your ride.

•The trail turns left and follows a chain-link fence back to the parking lot.

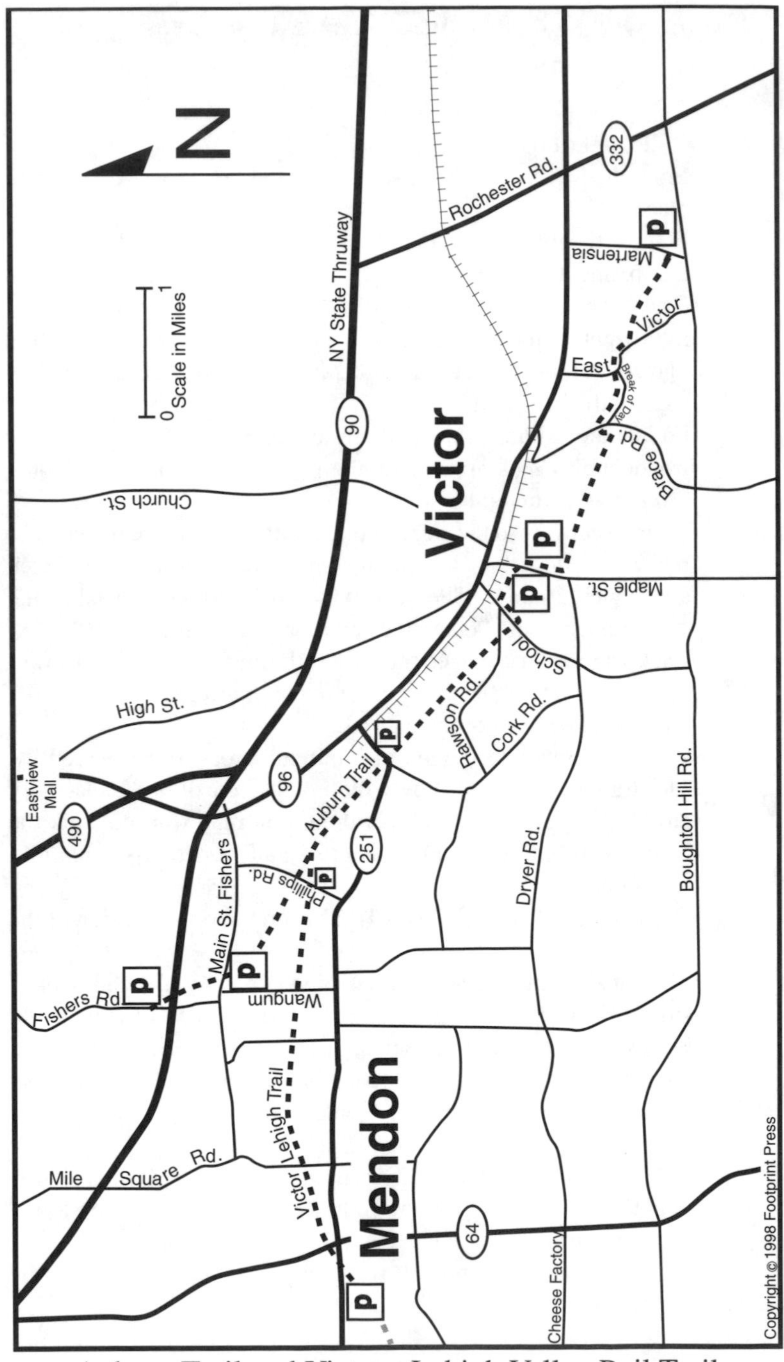

Auburn Trail and Victor - Lehigh Valley Rail Trail

15.

Auburn Trail

Location: Fishers Road, Victor, to Martensia Road, Farmington

Parking: Pull off at the trailhead on Fishers Road north of the Thruway at the green-and-yellow sign for "Victor Hiking Trails." There is room for only one car.

Alternative Parking: In back of the Fishers Firehouse on Main Street, Fishers

Victor Volunteer Fireman's Memorial Field, Maple Street, Victor

West side of Martensia Road at brown sign saying "Farmington - Welcome to Auburn Trail"

Riding Time: 65 minutes one way

Length: 7.5 miles one way

Difficulty: Easy, mostly level

Surface: Cinder and mowed-grass path

Trail Markings: 3.5-inch white, rectangular, metal markers for "Victor Hiking Trail"

11-inch green-and-yellow "Victor Hiking Trail" signs at road crossings

Brown signs for "Farmington - Welcome to Auburn Trail"

Uses:

Contact: Victor Hiking Trails, Inc.
85 East Main Street
Victor, NY 14564

The Auburn Trail was one of the first trails opened by Victor Hiking Trails. This volunteer group was conceived by the Victor Conservation Board in the 1980s. The first organizational meeting occurred in September 1991, and the Auburn Trail opened in September 1993. The eastern section of the Auburn Trail was developed and is maintained by the town of Farmington.

The Auburn Trail was once the bustling Rochester and Auburn Railroad. No rails or ties remain on the railroad bed; they have been gone for years. At one time, the Auburn was part of the New York Central Railroad System, owned by Cornelius Vanderbilt. It was the main east-west line.

Where the Auburn rail bed is not accessible in the village of Victor, this bikeway detours for a short distance on the old Rochester and Eastern Trolley bed. On your journey, you'll pass a train station from each of these lines. The trolley station will be directly in front of you as you cross Maple Street. The Auburn trail station is in the Whistle Stop Arcade.

You will also pass through a spectacular tunnel under the New York State Thruway. The tunnel was built large enough for trains. At another point two former railroads cross, so you will ride under an old railroad trestle which was used by the Lehigh Valley Railroad. The trestle is now part of the Victor - Lehigh Valley Rail Trail.

Nature is plentiful along the way. Part of the rail bed is raised to overlook beautiful swamp and pond areas. Look carefully as you pedal by, and you may be able to pick some blackberries for a quick snack. The trail abounds with birds, beaver, deer, and muskrats. Geese may even honk as you pass their pens.

Entering the tunnel under the New York State Thruway.

History will also surround you. Be sure to watch for the old potato storage building and old rail sidings as you pass through Fishers. Stop to admire the 1845, cobblestone, railroad pump house (adjacent to the Fishers firehouse). It's the oldest cobblestone railroad building in the country. Concrete "tombstones" along the way were mileposts for the trains. One marked "S85" denoted that Syracuse was 85 miles away. A "W" in the concrete marker told the engineer that a road crossing was coming and to blow the train's whistle. See if you can find a rectangular concrete box partly buried in the ballast. This battery box was used to power the signals at road crossings if the main power was down.

Please stay on the white-marked railway bed. Other trails intersect this path, but bikes are not permitted on them. There are some remaining "No Trespassing" signs along the way. As long as you stay on the old rail bed, you can ignore them. The rail bed is open for public use from Fishers Road to Brace Road and East Victor Road to Martensia Road.

The cobblestone pump house in the village of Fishers.

Mud Creek winds its way under the Auburn Trail.

Distances between main roads:

Fishers Road to Main Street, Fishers	0.6 mile
Main Street, Fishers to Phillips Road	0.9 mile
Phillips Road to Route 251	1.1 miles
Route 251 to Rawson Road	1.1 miles
Rawson Road to School Street	0.2 mile
School Street to Maple Street (via trolley)	0.6 mile
Maple Street to Whistle Stop	0.4 mile
Whistle Stop to Brace Road	1.2 miles
Brace Road to rail bed on E. Victor Road	0.8 mile
E. Victor Road to Martensia Road	0.6 mile

Trail Directions

•From the trailhead at Fishers Road, head southeast past a brown metal gate, on a mowed path.
•Geese may honk at you from their pen on the left.
•Pass through the tunnel under the New York State Thruway.
•Emerge from the woods along the side yard of a house.
•Cross Main Street, Fishers, and continue across the grass between the Fishers firehouse on your right and the cobblestone pump house on your left.
•A green-and-yellow "Victor Hiking Trails" sign directs you straight ahead, back into the woods.
•Notice the old potato storage building on your right. Look for the water ditch from the creek that was used by the cobblestone pump house.
•Ride around the metal gates on each side of Phillips Road.
•Ride under the old trestle for the Lehigh Valley Railroad. In the spring of 1998 a connecting path will be built to join the Auburn Trail with the Victor - Lehigh Trail (#16).
•Watch for the concrete battery box on the right and beaver in the creek to your left.
•The cinder path widens. Snapping turtles like to bury their eggs in the cinder banks.
•Pass the metal gates and cross Route 251 (Victor-Mendon Road).
•A red marker for Seneca Trail is on the left. Bikes are not permitted on Seneca Trail.
•The Seneca Trail (red markers) intersects again.
•Pass the metal gates and cross Rawson Road.
•Turn left onto School Street. (The trail ahead turns into Seneca Trail and heads south toward Ganondagan National Historic Site. It is open to walkers only.)
•Just after the post office, the path turns to asphalt.
•Turn right to stay on the asphalt path.
•Cross active railroad tracks, then a wooden bridge.
•Arrive on Maple Street at the Victor Volunteer Fireman's Memorial Field sign. Parking is available here. Directly across

Maple Street is the old trolley station, now a business. Downtown Victor and shops are to the left.

•Turn right (S) on Maple Street. Sidewalks are available on both sides of this busy road.

•Pass stately old homes along Maple Street. Pass East Street.

•Turn left onto the railroad bed just after the sign for the Whistle Stop Arcade. The former Rochester and Auburn train station is on your left.

•Cross through Mickey Finn's Restaurant parking lot toward a metal gate with a "No Motor Vehicles" sign.

•Cross a new housing development road. Ride through a wooded area.

•Victor Hills Golf Course is on the right.

•Turn left onto Brace Road. (The trail ahead, between Brace and East Victor Roads, is a narrow path through close trees. Bikes are not allowed.)

•At the stop sign, turn right onto Break Of Day Road.

•Turn right onto East Victor Road and head uphill.

•Watch for a yellow-and-green "Hiking Trail" sign on the left, just before the power lines that cross East Victor Road, and turn left onto the trail bed.

•Negotiate some tight turns then a roller-coaster ride on a raised cinder bed.

•Pass a brown sign saying "Farmington - Welcome to Auburn Trail."

•Cross a bridge with chain-link sides over Mud Creek.

•Notice the gorgeous view of the rock strewn creek to your right. In the spring, look for bluebells.

•A cement pillar "S82" is hidden in the brush on the right (W) side of the trail. This told the train engineer that it was 82 miles to Syracuse.

•The public trail ends at Martensia Road with parking available.

16.

Victor - Lehigh Valley Rail Trail

Location: Phillips Road, Victor, to the village of Mendon (see map on page 100)

Parking: Along Phillips Road. Make sure that you park at the trail crossing closest to Victor-Mendon Road. The trail crossing just to the north is the Auburn Trail.

Alternative Parking: At the Honeoye Falls - Mendon Youth Baseball Field on Route 251 just west of the four corners in Mendon (across from Ye Mendon Tavern)

Riding Time: 30 minutes one way

Length: 2.8 miles one way

Difficulty: Easy, mostly level

Surface: Cinder, dirt, gravel, and mowed grass path

Trail Markings: 11-inch green-and-yellow "Victor Hiking Trail" signs at road crossings

Uses: 

Contact: Victor Hiking Trails, Inc.
85 East Main Street
Victor, NY 14564

Here's another new trail to explore, thanks to a cooperative effort. The Victor-Lehigh Rail Trail used to be deep in ballast stone, but in the winter of 1997, the Victor Department of Transportation graded the path to plow away most of the ballast. Eastman Kodak

Company donated fly ash for the treadway. Monroe County installed the fly ash and supplied signs. Coordination and maintenance are being provided by Victor Hiking Trails.

The easternmost end connects with the Auburn Trail (#15) where the Lehigh Railroad trestle passes high over the Auburn line. At its western end, it continues past the village of Mendon for 12.5 miles, to the Genesee River as the Mendon - Lehigh Valley Rail Trail (#17).

The Lehigh Valley Railroad got its start in the coal mines of Pennsylvania. Valleys cut by the Lehigh River became channels for transporting the inexpensive, high-grade, anthracite or hard coal from the mines to Rochester and Buffalo. The Rochester station still stands on Court Street across from the Rundel Library.

The Lehigh Valley Railroad was built in 1891 to capture some of the lucrative "black diamond" (as coal was nicknamed) freight business. The train, dubbed the "Black Diamond Express," was advertised as the "Handsomest Train in the World." In 1896 it began passenger service between Buffalo and New York. This plush train offered smoking rooms, a polished mahogany library, velvet upholstery, and beveled French-plate mirrors. The engine was an iron horse manufactured by Baldwin. It could reach speeds of 80 miles per hour and maintained its schedule 92% of the time. Honeymooners often rode in luxury to Niagara Falls.

In the 1920s anthracite coal began to lose favor as a home-heating fuel. Homeowners discovered the ease and low cost of gas and oil. By the 1930s the Depression and competition from cars and trucks steadily pulled business away from the trains. Ownership of the rail line changed several times until 1974 when the business was dismantled for scrap iron and parts.

Distances between major roads:

Phillips Road to Wangum Road	0.7 mile
Wangum Road to Old Dutch Road	0.4 mile
Old Dutch Road to Mile Square Road	1.0 mile
Mile Square Road to Route 64	0.6 mile
Route 64 to Route 251	0.1 mile

Trail Directions

•From Phillips Road head west along the newly resurfaced rail bed.

•Cross Wangum Road, former site of Fisherville.

•Cross Old Dutch Road. In 0.5 mile there will be a short stretch of ballast stone. Then the path will turn to cinder.

•Cross Mile Square Road.

•Ride across a redecked bridge over Irondequoit Creek. The path will become mowed grass.

•Cross Route 64. The path returns to cinder and gravel.

•Cross a small creek.

•Cross Route 251. Parking is available here. The trail does continue on to the Genesee River. See the Mendon - Lehigh Valley Rail Trail (#17).

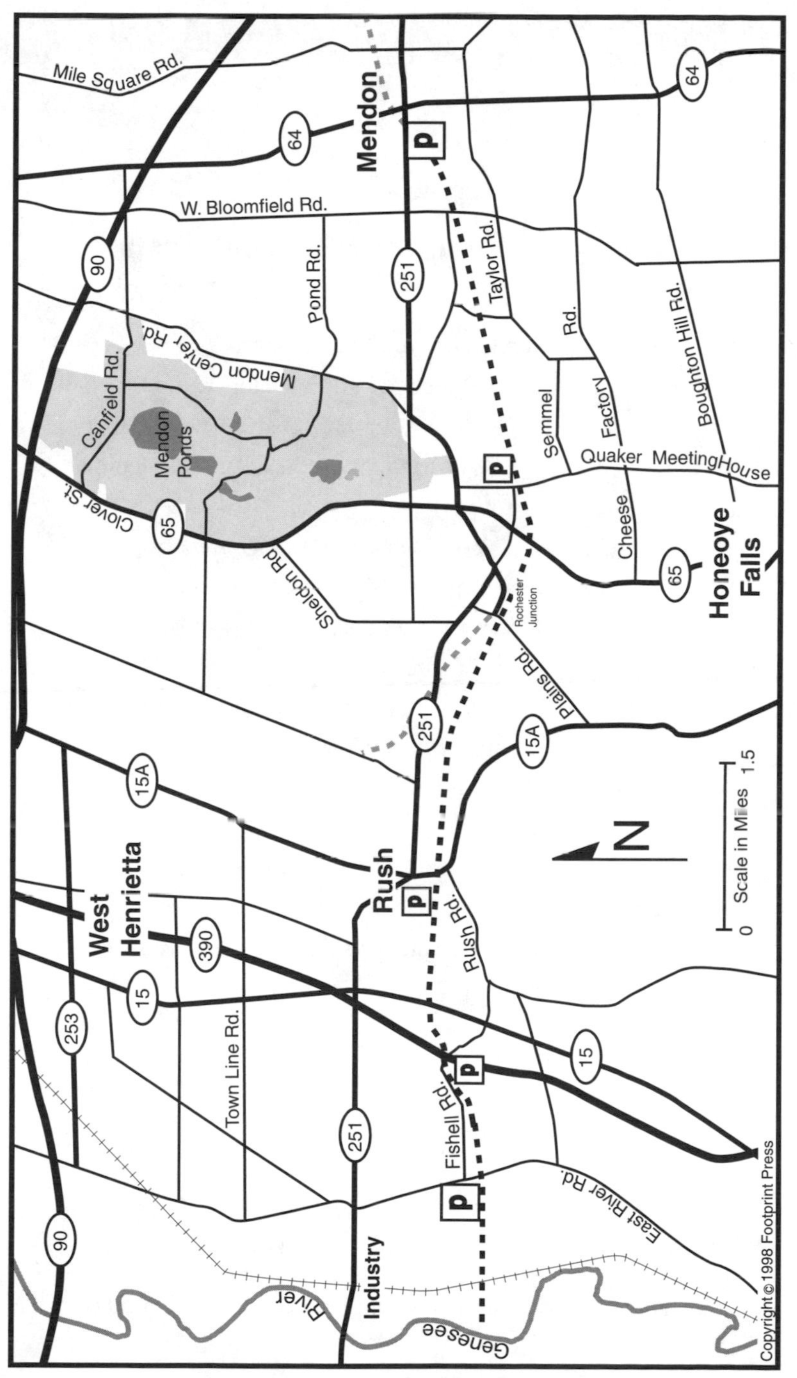

Mendon - Lehigh Valley Rail Trail

17.
Mendon - Lehigh Valley Rail Trail

Location: Mendon to the Genesee River

Parking: At the Honeoye Falls-Mendon Youth Baseball Field on Route 251, just west of the four corners of Mendon (across from Ye Mendon Tavern)

Alternative Parking: East side of Quaker Meeting House Road
Rush Veterans Memorial Park, Route 15A, Rush
Honeoye Creek Fishing Access, Fishell Road, under Interstate 390
East River Road, south of Fishell Road, Rush (potential endpoint)

Riding Time: 1 hour and 45 minutes one way

Length: 12.5 miles one way

Difficulty: Difficult, mostly level, bumpy ride

Surface: Cinder and stone

Trail Markings: Only signs stating "No Motorized Vehicles"

Uses:

Contact: The Mendon Foundation
P.O. Box 231
Mendon, NY 14506

The Mendon - Lehigh Valley Rail Trail is for the rough and ready. The Mendon Foundation is three years into their five-year, trail development plan. A new cinder surface, additional bridges, drainage repairs, and signs are all planned. The current trail has a stony bed which makes for a bumpy ride, dirt mounds at the road crossings that any BMX rider will enjoy, and puddles to splash through. But, don't pass up this ride if you want country solitude through woods and fields, because this path has that also. It offers a welcome escape from the clutter and noise of urban Rochester.

The Lehigh Valley Railroad got its start in the coal mines of Pennsylvania. Valleys cut by the Lehigh River became channels for transporting the inexpensive, high-grade, anthracite or hard coal from the mines to Rochester and Buffalo. The Rochester station still stands on Court Street across from the Rundel Library. Rochester Junction in Mendon was a major intersection where trains ran west to Buffalo, south to Hemlock Lake, and north to Rochester. Remains of the old rail station platform are visible today.

The Lehigh Valley Railroad was built in 1891 to capture some of the lucrative "black diamond" (as coal was nicknamed) freight business. The train, dubbed the "Black Diamond Express," was advertised as the "Handsomest Train in the World." In 1896 it began passenger service between Buffalo and New York. This plush train offered smoking rooms, a polished-mahogany library, velvet upholstery, and beveled French-plate mirrors. The engine was an iron horse manufactured by Baldwin. It could reach speeds of 80 miles per hour and maintained its schedule 92% of the time. Honeymooners often rode in luxury to Niagara Falls.

In the 1920s anthracite coal began to lose favor as a home-heating fuel. Homeowners discovered the ease and low cost of gas and oil. By the 1930s the Depression and competition from cars and trucks steadily pulled business away from the trains. Ownership of the rail line changed several times until 1974 when the business was dismantled for scrap iron and parts. Today the county of Monroe owns the railroad bed. The trail is being developed by the towns of Mendon and Rush, the Monroe County Parks Department, and especially a non-profit land trust organization called Mendon Foundation and many volunteers. As you ride this trail, think back

A newly redecked bridge over Honeoye Creek.

to the times when steam locomotives hauled coal, and the "Black Diamond" transported passengers in luxury. Keep your eyes to the ground, and you may be lucky enough to find a piece of "black diamond" from a bygone era.

The Mendon Foundation is using an innovative program to beautify the road intersections of the Lehigh Valley Trail. Their "Adopt an Intersection" program gives landscapers advertising opportunities in exchange for planting and caring for vegetation where the trail crosses roads. Likewise, they've solicited donations from residents for beautification of the Route 251 parking lot. This is certainly a win/win situation that benefits the whole community.

This trail extends east from Route 251, ending in Victor. Connect the route described here with the Victor - Lehigh Valley Rail Trail (#16) for a 15.3 mile adventure (one way).

Distances between parking areas:

Route 251 to Quaker Meeting House Road	3.4 miles
Quaker Meeting House Road to Route 15A	4.5 miles
Route 15A to Fishell Road	1.9 miles
Fishell Road to East River Road	1.3 miles

Trail Directions

•From the Route 251 parking lot, head southwest past wooden posts on a cinder and stone path.
•Cross a small cement bridge over a creek.
•Cross West Bloomfield Road.
•Walk or ride over a dirt mound and through a short stretch of ballast stone.
•Parallel Irondequoit Creek on your left for a short while.
•Cross Chamberlain Road.
•Traverse several short sections of ballast stone.
•Ride around and through a series of wet areas and cross another dirt mound.
•Cross Quaker Meeting House Road.
•Wind down a mowed path, cross a small stream, and climb to cross Route 65. (Parking is not available at Route 65.)
•Note the old railroad bridge to your left as an abandoned Conrail line merges with the Lehigh.
•On the right pass an old cement platform and switching mechanism. This area was once Rochester Junction where the Lehigh and Conrail trains crossed.
•Cross Plains Road. (Junction Road is visible to the north.)
(Side Trip: Just past the white house [275 Plains Road] another railroad bed heads northwest for 0.9 mile to a parking area along Route 251. The trail north of Route 251 is cleared for 1.8 miles, but deep pumice stones make it impassable for bicycles.)
•Cross over a large metal trestle bridge spanning Honeoye Creek. This bridge has new decking and railings spanning 160 feet, compliments of Boy Scout Troop 45 of Rochester, The Monroe County Parks Department, and Mendon Foundation volunteers.

•Emerge onto Park Lane. Honeoye Creek is on your right. There is a picnic area at Rush Veterans Memorial Park.
(Note: A quarter mile to the right (N) are a grocery store and a convenience store at the corner of Route 251.)
•Cross Route 15A next to Rush Creekside Inn. You've come 8 miles so far.
•Cross a second trestle bridge over Honeoye Creek. This 120-foot span was redecked by volunteers from the village of Rush.
•Ride under the Route 15 bridge.
•The trail bends left, parallel to Interstate 390.
•Head downhill to Fishell Road.
•Turn right and ride under Interstate 390, past Honeoye Creek Fishing Access.
•Shortly after the Interstate 390 bridge, bear left and head uphill on a gravel path.
•Cross a driveway.
•Cross East River Road. This is the last parking area along the trail. Beyond this point the bridges have not been resurfaced. If you continue the remaining 1.3 miles to the Genesee River, use caution. Also, this area is not recommended for children. Future plans include extending this trail over the Genesee River to connect with the Genesee Valley Greenway.
•Cross a bridge over the Conrail tracks. The bridge is passable but not redecked, use caution.
•Cross a bridge over a swamp. The bridge is passable but not redecked, use caution.
•Pass a large stone abutment. A large trestle used to span from this point, over the Genesee River.
•Head downhill and the path becomes a narrow mowed strip through woods.
•The trail ends at the old bridge over the Genesee River. This bridge is not passable.

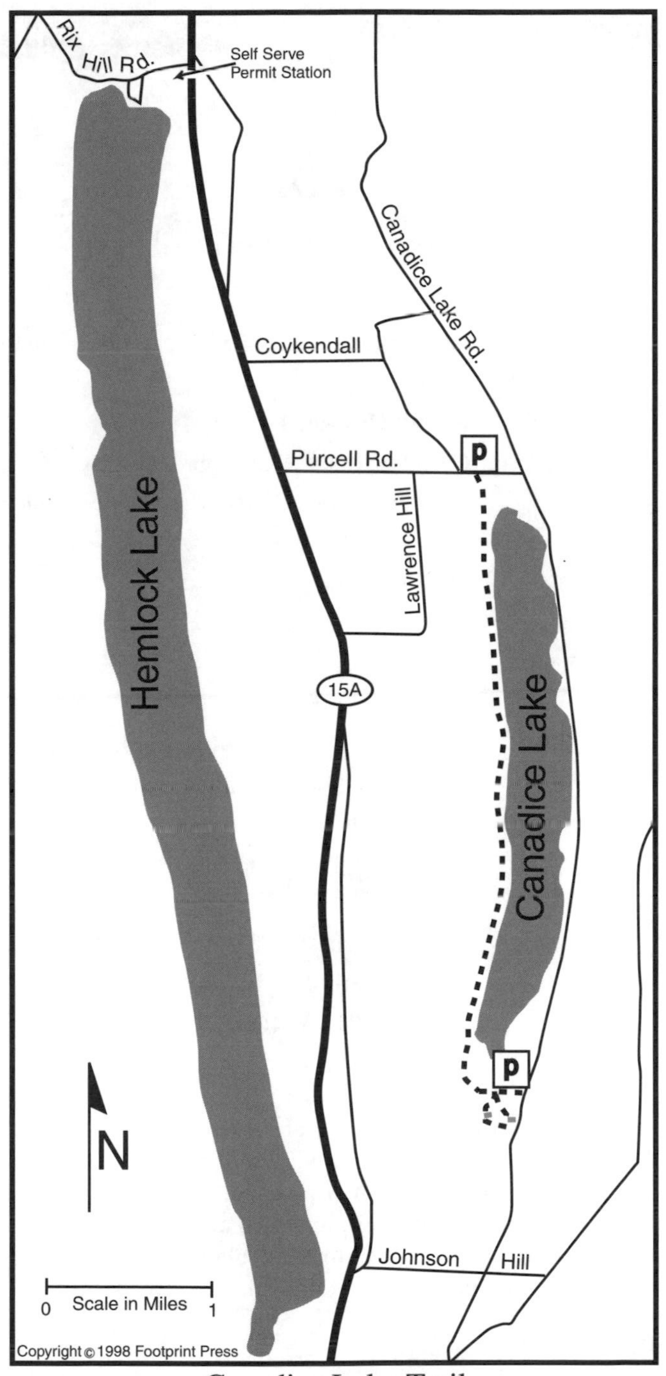

Canadice Lake Trail

18.

Canadice Lake Trail

Location: West side of Canadice Lake, going north to south

Parking: Purcell Hill Road

Alternative Parking: Canadice Lake Road, approximately 3.5 miles south of Purcell Hill Road on west side of road (lake side)

Riding Time: 35 minutes one way

Length: 3.7 miles one way

Difficulty: Easy, mostly level

Surface: Two lane, gravel, grass

Trail Markings: 12 x 18-inch, green-and-white signs labeled with hiker silhouettes and "Hemlock Canadice Watershed"

Uses: 

Contact: City of Rochester, Water and Lighting Bureau
7412 Rix Hill Road
Hemlock, NY 14466
(716) 346-2617

Long ago, Canadice Lake had cottages all along its shore. In 1872 the city of Rochester decided to use Canadice and Hemlock Lakes as a water supply. The first conduit for water was completed in 1876. By 1947 Rochester purchased all of the shoreline property and removed the cottages so that it could preserve the water supply for its growing population. Although it was very difficult for the cottage residents to leave their land, this area is now free of the commercialization that is so rampant on the other Finger Lakes. Ninety-foot-deep Canadice Lake is the smallest of the Finger Lakes, but it has the highest elevation, at 1,096 feet, one of the reasons it is such a good water supply for the city. Flow from Canadice Outlet Creek is diverted into the northern end of Hemlock Lake. From there the City of Rochester Water Bureau conditions the water for drinking and sends it north via large pipes.

Early settlers tried to farm around Canadice Lake but found the glacially scoured land ill-suited for farming. Many areas around the lake were too steep or too wet for growing crops.

Today, the Hemlock and Canadice Lakes watershed continues to be Rochester's primary source of drinking water. The watershed covers more than 40,000 acres of land, of which Rochester owns 7,000 acres. A second-growth forest now prospers on the once forested land, and many abandoned farm fields have been reforested with conifers. Bald eagles are now present in the area.

The serene Canadice Lake Trail.

To protect city property and the supply of drinking water, the city asks that all visitors obtain a Watershed Visitor Permit, one of the easiest permits to obtain. Just stop at the visitor's self-serve, permit station located at the north end of Hemlock Lake on Rix Hill Road off Route 15A. There are no fees or forms to fill out, but the permit document details the dos and don'ts to help keep the area pristine, so it's important to read it. Swimming and camping are not permitted. Boats up to 16 feet long with motors up to 10 horsepower are okay. The permit also has a detailed map showing additional hiking trails.

You may also want to continue west on Rix Hill Road to beautiful Hemlock Lake Park, which has restrooms, a pavilion with grills, and even a gazebo. The exceptionally well-managed watershed area contains a variety of trees, including hemlock, beech, oak, maple, hickory, basswood, and white, red and scotch pine. In addition, if you care to fish, the lake has salmon, trout, and panfish. Or try your hand at birdwatching. You may see kingfishers, herons, ospreys, as well as bald eagles near the water. The relatively undisturbed forest along the trail is ideal habitat for several woodpecker species. Also, the narrow lake and forested shoreline create excellent sighting opportunities for spring and autumn migrating warblers and other songbirds.

Trail Directions

- From the parking area, head south past the gate. The trail, an abandoned town road, meanders back and forth through oak, maple, tulip poplar, and conifer trees, but is never very far from the lake. See if you can spot the old cottage foundations along the way.
- At the end of the lake, the trail turns left (E) onto gravel.
- At the bench you have a choice. You can continue straight and soon arrive at another gated trail entrance off of Canadice Lake Road, or you can turn right to explore a circle trail with a bench in the center. Off the circle is another trail that also takes you to Canadice Lake Road.

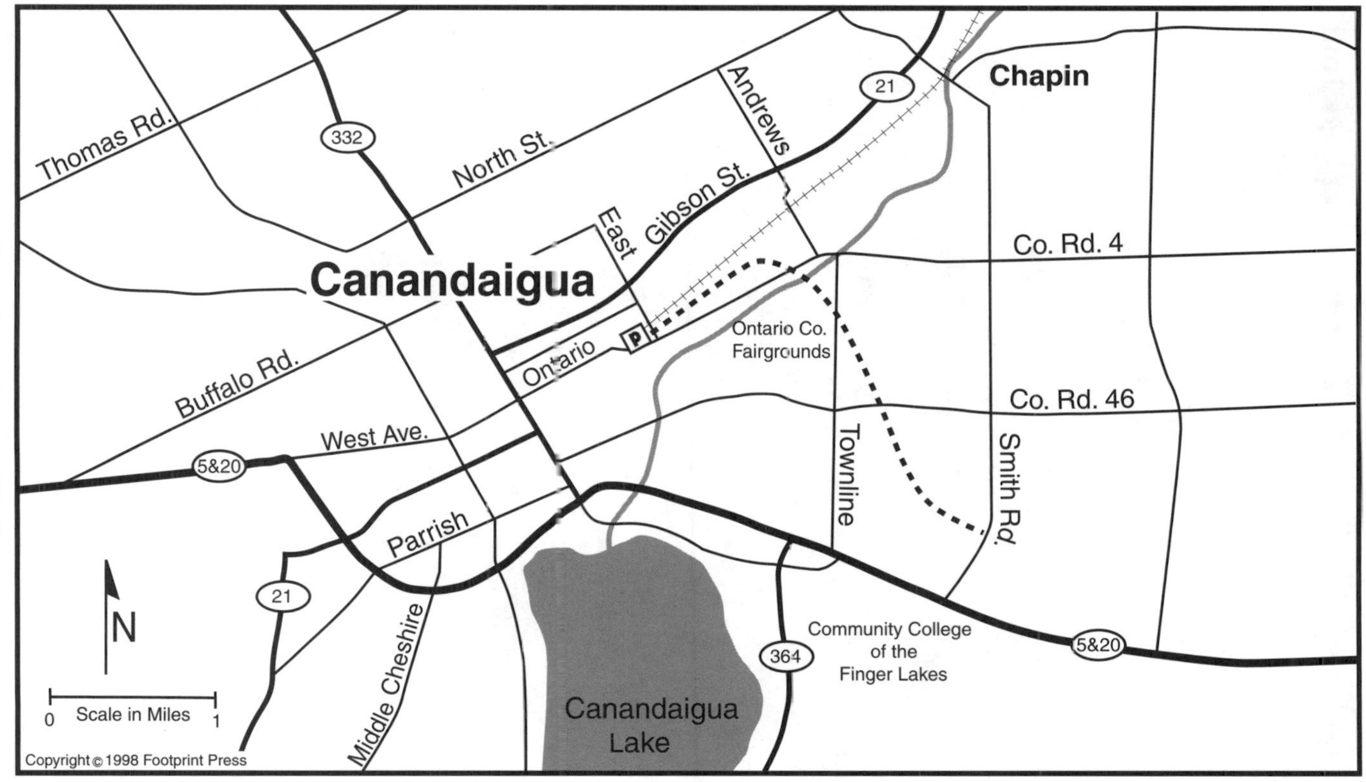

Ontario Pathways Trail

19.

Ontario Pathways Trail

Location: Ontario Street to Smith Road, Canandaigua

Parking: To find the parking lot on Ontario Street, head south on Route 332. Turn left onto Ontario Street just after the Ontario County Courthouse (a yellow building with a statue on its gold-domed roof). Pass the Ontario County Sheriff and Jail building. Cross active railroad tracks. The parking lot is on the left in front of an old red warehouse.

Alternative Parking: None

Riding Time: 30 minutes one way

Length: 3.4 miles one way

Difficulty: Easy, mostly level

Surface: Cinder and mowed grass

Trail Markings: Plastic, green-and-white signs that read "Welcome to Ontario Pathways"

Uses: 

Contact: Ontario Pathways
Betsy Russell
P.O. Box 996
Canandaigua, NY 14424
(716) 394-7968

Ontario Pathways is a grass-roots organization, formed in 1993 of people dedicated to the establishment of public-access trails throughout Ontario County. They purchased and are working to develop two rail beds abandoned by the Penn Central Corporation. Trains last thundered over this land in 1972 when Hurricane Agnes hit and damaged many of the rails. When complete, these two rail beds will cover 22 miles from Canandaigua southwest to Stanley, and from Stanley north to Phelps. Two other mile-long stretches of the Ontario Pathways trail are open for public use in addition to the 3.4 miles described here.

The rail bed you'll be riding started operation in 1851 as the Canandaigua Corning Line and was financed by prominent Canandaigua residents Mark Sibley, John Granger, Oliver Phelps III, and Jared Wilson. But this short line, like many of its cousins, suffered grave financial losses and changed names four times in 14 years. Even the federal government became involved when, in 1862, President Abe Lincoln authorized the expenditure of $50,000 to revive the line so that men and supplies could be moved southward to the Civil War battlefront in Pennsylvania. Recruits rode this

For a short distance the trail parallels active railroad tracks.

line to training centers in Elmira, New York, and Harrisburg, Pennsylvania.

By 1880 Canandaigua became a tourist attraction. Cargo switched from agricultural goods to passengers, as five trains ran daily between Canandaigua and Elmira. But, as with all of the railroads, business faded in the 1950s and 60s because of competition from cars and trucks. The rail line changed hands many more times, until the merger of Northern Central with New York Central to form the Penn Central in 1968. Penn Central filed for bankruptcy in 1970, and train traffic dwindled even further. When Hurricane Agnes blew through the area in 1972, she damaged bridges, tracks, and rail beds. Penn Central abandoned the line, sold the rails for scrap, and sold the land corridor.

The trail is an easy-riding, 10-foot-wide swath through beautiful countryside. We rode it in the fall, pedaling over a bed of colored leaves with the canopy above blazing reds and yellows. It would be a delight to ride this trail in any season, except of course, in snow season.

Bike Shop: Park Avenue Bike Shop, Parkway Plaza, Route 5 and 20, (716) 398-2300

Distance between major roads:

Ontario Street to East Street	0.3 mile
East Street to Ontario Street	0.9 mile
Ontario Street to Townline Road	0.4 mile
Townline Road to County Road 46	0.8 mile
County Road 46 to Smith Road	1.0 mile

An enjoyable canopy of colored leaves in the fall and shade in the summer.

Trail Directions

•From the parking lot head northeast on the trail, away from the city of Canandaigua, parallel to an active set of railroad tracks. If you're lucky, a train will come by.
•Cross East Street.
•Pass a red metal gate. On the left, watch for the cement pillar with "S73" denoting 73 miles to Syracuse.
•After awhile, the trail and railroad tracks diverge.
•Head downhill past a red gate. Cross Ontario Street.
•Head uphill then cross a long wooden bridge over Canandaigua Outlet.
•The Ontario County Fair Grounds appears on your right.
•Cross Townline Road near the entrance to the Fair Grounds.
•Cross County Road 46. You've now come 2.4 miles.
•Cross a dirt driveway.
•The trail ends at Smith Road. A red gate across the street says "Do Not Enter." Turn around and retrace your path.

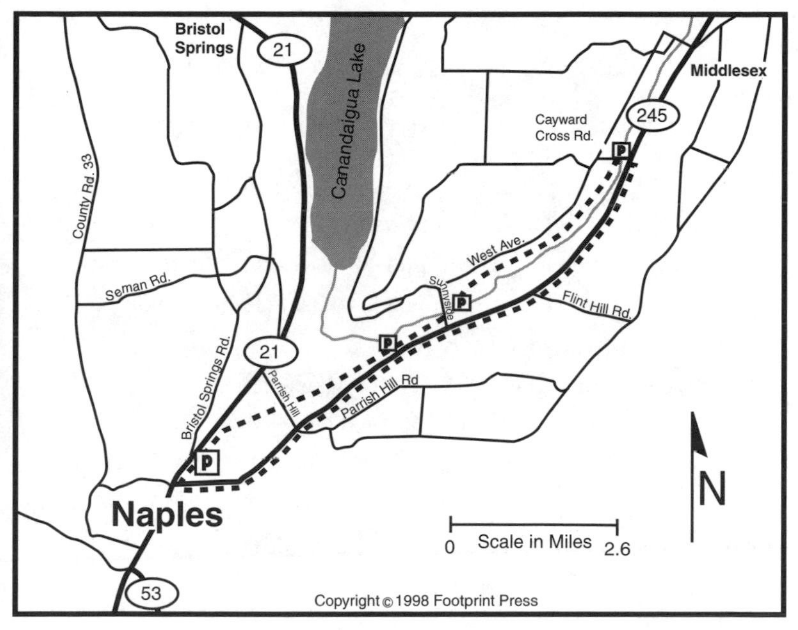

Middlesex Valley Railroad Trail

20.

Middlesex Valley Railroad Trail

Location: Hi-Tor area, Naples

Parking: Large, dirt, pull-off area along Route 21, just north of Naples, past the intersection of County Road 12

Alternative Parking: Route 245, Hi-Tor Management Area - West River Unit (boat launch)

Sunnyside Road off Route 245, West River Fishing Access

Trail's endpoint at Cayward Cross Road, off Route 245

Riding Time: 1 hour one way

If you return on roads, the round trip is 1.6 hours (14.6 miles round trip)

Length: 6.8 miles one way

Difficulty: Moderate, level with gradual uphill

Surface: Mowed grass

Trail Markings: None

Uses:

Contact: Bob & Holly Elwell
6974 Reservoir Road
Naples, NY 14512
(716) 374-5554

New York State Department of Environmental
Conservation
6274 Avon-Lima Road
Avon, NY 14414
(716) 226-2466

Don't let the fact that this is an old rail bed fool you into thinking it's an easy ride. As you pedal north, you don't notice a grade. But the pedaling is tough as the trail goes steadily uphill. This ride is well worth the effort, however, because you'll find scenery that you won't see on any other rail trail. You'll ride through Middlesex Valley with the towering hills of Naples on either side.

Most of the rail bed is a raised platform through a wetland. But, because it passes through wetlands, it may be impassable in wet weather.

One of several bridges to cross on the Middlesex Valley Railroad Trail.

Along the way are waterfowl nesting boxes; and about one mile southwest of Cayward Cross Road is a blue heron rookery. Please be quiet and don't disturb the birds.

The official name of this trail is the Lehigh Valley Rail Trail. But since other sections of the Lehigh are open for biking and hiking, we've called it by its historical name. The Middlesex Valley Railroad first provided service between Naples and Stanley in 1892. The line was later extended to Geneva. In 1895 the rail line was purchased by the Lehigh Valley Railroad. Service continued until 1970 when the line was abandoned due to competition from trucks and cars for the freight of coal, building materials, farm equipment, apples, grapes, beans, etc. Most of the land reverted to private ownership. This portion of the rail trail is owned by New York State as part of the Hi-Tor Game Management Area. It is a public hunting ground, so avoid hunting season.

Distance between major roads:

Route 21 to Parish Hill	1.2 miles
Parish Hill to Sunnyside	2.6 miles
Sunnyside to Cayward Cross	3.0 miles

A great trail for birdwatching.

Trail Directions

- •Head toward the yellow metal gate and stop sign onto a 12 foot wide, mowed-grass path.
- •Cross the first of many wooden bridges over a creek.
- •Emerge from the woods to a vineyard, then a field on your right. The Naples hills tower above as a backdrop to the fields.
- •Continue parallel to the creek.
- •Cross the second wooden bridge. These bridges were repaired by the NY State Department of Environmental Conservation.
- •Pass a yellow metal gate then cross Parish Hill Road.
- •Pass another yellow metal gate and ride through a raised bed over wetlands.
- •Cross the third wooden bridge. Here are some short sections of ballast stone.
- •Cross the forth wooden bridge, then a few more short sections of ballast.
- •The trail now runs parallel to a road.

•Cross the fifth wooden bridge.
•Pass through a backyard of farm animals. This is home to a horse, donkey, lamb, and goat as well as many ducks, geese, guinea fowl, turkeys, chickens, and rabbits. The front of this home is a roadside farm stand which sells produce, tarts, pies, breads, snacks, and drinks.
•Pass through another yellow gate into the parking area and boat launch for Hi-Tor Management Area - West River Unit.
•Head toward the first yellow gate.
•Pass more yellow gates.
•Pass the West River Fishing Access site. The West River is on your left. Across the river is the legendary site of the first Seneca Indian village, Nundawao.
•Cross Sunnyside Road. You've ridden 3.8 miles so far.
•Pass yellow gates.
•Cross a long wooden bridge where the waters fork. Trailers are on the left, then a beaver dam and dens on the right.
•Cross the seventh wooden bridge. Enjoy wetlands on both sides of the path.
•Continue on a long stretch through a wooded area.
•The land again turns to wetlands, this time with clumps of wild daylilies along the shore.
•The path ends at the yellow gates at Cayward Cross Road. From here you have two options. One is to turnaround and follow the rail trail back to the start. The other is to follow the roads back. The roads have good paved shoulders and are predominately downhill. Turn right (E) onto Cayward Cross Road, right onto Route 245, then right again when it ends at Route 21. This takes you back to the start. Along the way, pass an old cemetery and a roadside farm stand.

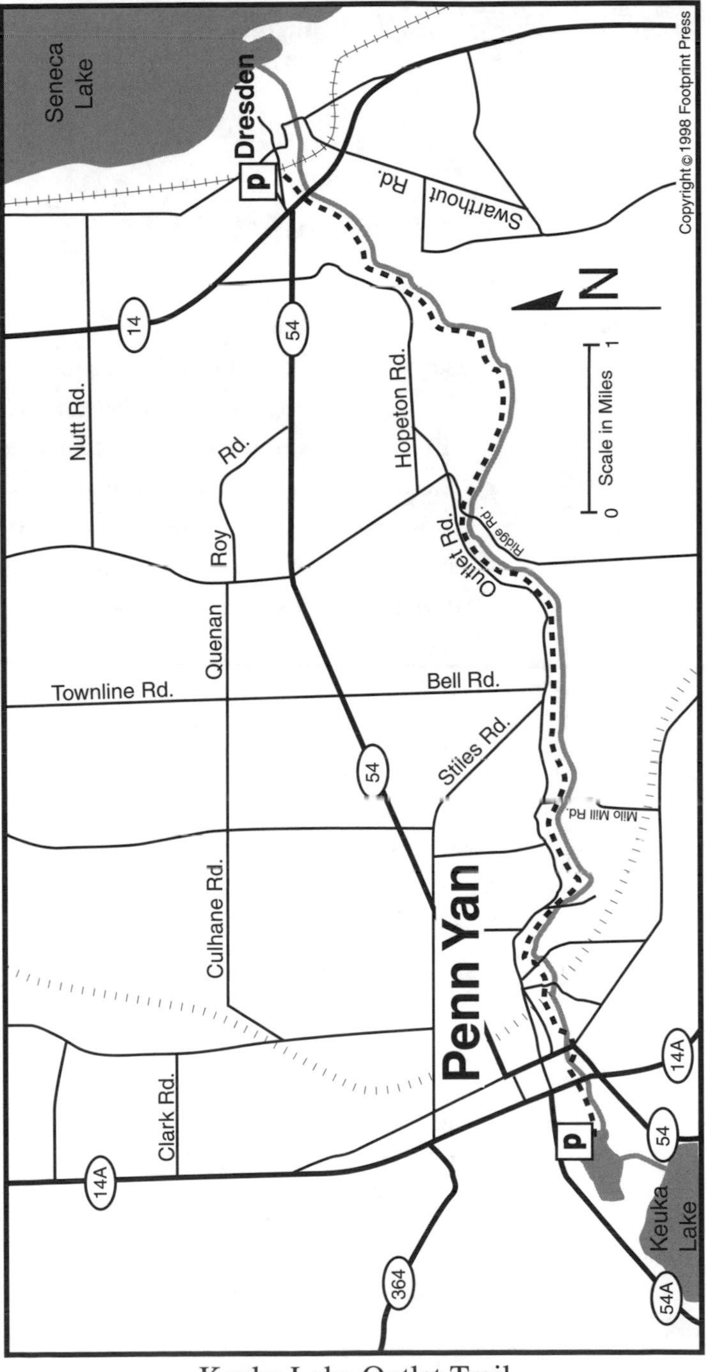

Keuka Lake Outlet Trail

21.

Keuka Lake Outlet Trail

Location: Dresden to Penn Yan, Yates County

Parking: Dresden, half way down on the west side of Seneca Lake. From Route 14 south, turn left (E) at Route 54 heading toward Main Street, Dresden. There is a Citgo gas station and the Crossroads Ice Cream Shop at the corner. At the Crossroads Ice Cream Shop take an immediate right onto Seneca Street. Parking is on your right just before the railroad tracks.

Alternative Parking: Penn Yan, Marsh Development Project, Little League Baseball, on Route 54A (Elm Street)

Riding Time: 1.25 hours one way

Length: 7.5 miles one way

Difficulty: Easy, mostly flat, some small hills

Surface: Dirt (western end is paved)

Trail Markings: None, easy-to-follow trail

Uses:

Contact: Friends of the Finger Lakes Outlet
PO Box 231
Penn Yan, NY 14527

The strip of land you will be biking from Seneca Lake to Keuka Lake is steeped in history. You'll see the evidence of places and events from several bygone eras as you pedal westward.

In the middle of the nineteenth century, two fingers of water connected the 274-foot drop between Keuka and Seneca Lakes, the outlet to power mills, and the Crooked Lake Canal for boat traffic. A dam and guardhouse in Penn Yan controlled the water flow to both. The outlet, which still carries water from one lake to the next, was formed by a ground fault in the Tully limestone allowing water to run between the two lakes. Along its banks you'll see remnants of the many mills which once harnessed the water power.

The first white settlers arrived in this area around 1788, attracted by the reliable water source at the outlet. In 1789 Seneca Mill was built along the raging waters of Keuka Lake outlet to grind flour with a 26-foot, overshot flywheel. From then until 1827, a small religious group called the Society of Universal Friends built 12 dams and many mills that helped make the area a thriving community. The mills and shops produced flour (gristmills), lumber (sawmills), tool handles, linseed oil, plaster, and liquor (distilleries). There were two triphammer forges, eight fulling and carding mills, tanneries, and weavers making cotton and wool cloth. By 1835, thirty to forty mills were in operation. But, by 1900, only five mills remained, mainly making paper from straw. The last water-turbine mill ceased operation in 1968.

In 1833 New York State opened the Crooked Lake Canal to span the six miles between the two lakes and move farm products to eastern markets. The canal was four feet deep and had 28 wooden locks. It took a vessel six hours to journey through the canal. As business boomed in the mills, the state widened and deepened the canal and replaced the wooden locks with stone. But, the canal lost money every year of its 44-year history, so in 1877, the state auctioned off all of the machinery and stone. Only the towpath remained.

In 1844 a railroad was built on the towpath. Initially operated by the Penn Yan and New York Railway Company, it eventually became part of the New York Central System. Railway men called it the "Corkscrew Railway" because of its countless twists and turns. The line operated until 1972 when the tracks were washed out by the flood from Hurricane Agnes.

A local group interested in recreational use of the ravine convinced the town of Penn Yan to buy the property in 1981. Since then, it has been developed and maintained by a volunteer group called the Friends of the Outlet.

Bike Rentals: Crossroads Ice Cream Shop, Dresden [$10 per day, call for reservations (315) 531-5311]

Reference Guides: Purchase an illustrated guide to the Keuka Lake Outlet for $1.00 from the Yates County Historian, 110 Court Street, Penn Yan, NY 14527.

A packet of information on the history of the mill sites, canal, and railroad of the Keuka Lake Outlet is available for $3.00 at stores in Penn Yan.

Distances between major roads:

Seneca Street to Ridge Road	2.6 miles
Ridge Road to Milo Mill Road	1.8 miles
Milo Mill Road to Fox Mill Road	1.1 miles
Fox Mill Road to Cherry Street	0.1 mile
Cherry Street to Main Street	0.9 mile
Main Street to Route 54A	1.0 mile

Trail Directions

- The trail leads downhill from the back-right corner of the Dresden parking lot, heading west.
- Cross under the Route 14 bridge. The land you're on used to be the Dresden Mill Pond.

- •The wetland to your right (north of the trail) is the old Crooked Lake Canal.
- •Cross two wooden bridges
- •Notice the steep cliffs on both sides. Here where the canal and outlet are close together was the location of Lock 3. Watch for the cement and rebar millstone.
- •Cross a dirt road. This was Hopeton Road which, in the 1790s, connected Geneva to Bath through the town of Hopeton. To your left you can still see remnants of the iron-pony, truss bridge over the outlet. The bridge was built in 1840 and rests on stone abutments. This area was once a community of mills.
- •Hopeton Grist Mill was located just beyond the dirt road on the left. Nothing remains of it today.
- •On your left is a pleasant rest area with large rocks that you can sit on along the water.
- •Across the outlet, Bruces Gully cascades water over three waterfalls to join the outlet. Eventually the Friends of the Outlet plan to build a hiking trail through the gully. The dark gray rock, which peels in thin layers, is Genesee shale.
- •Pass a cement pillar on your right. The big "W" on the pillar signaled the train conductor to blow his whistle.
- •At the two-mile point are the remains of the J.T. Baker Chemical Company, manufacturers of the pesticide carbine bisulfide until 1968. At one time, this was also the site of a gristmill and several paper mills.
- •Here you'll see your first waterfall. The top step of the falls was the old dam, constructed in 1827 and the last of the 12 dams to be built along the outlet. Both Cascade Mill and Mallory's Mill used the water that was held back by this dam.
- •Follow the wide gravel path through the building area.
- •Pass old Kelly Tire buildings. These buildings were recently renovated into the Alfred Jensen Memorial Visitor Center by the Friends of the Outlet. It's a good place to stop if you need a restroom.
- •Follow the green-and-white trail signs as the trail branches to the left.

•Cross the paved Ridge Road. In 1805 May's Mills stood at this site. It had a gristmill, a sawmill, and a post office. In the 1820s this area was home to a cotton factory, then a distillery.

•Continue along the outlet. Outlet Road parallels close to the trail.

•Just over a culvert is another cement post displaying a "W," then another cement marker with "D3" which told the conductor that Dresden was 3 miles away. This means that you're almost halfway to Penn Yan.

•Pass a parking lot off Outlet Road. The brick remnants on the right were once a factory that turned rags into paper.

•Look for the large rock between the bike path and the outlet. A plaque on the side facing the outlet commemorates John Sheridan, a lawyer who negotiated the purchase of land for the Keuka Lake outlet preservation area. The stone remnants across the outlet were once a forge. At one time a road crossed over the dam at this spot. Seneca Mill, the first mill site, was located at this falls, the largest falls on the outlet.

•On your right (away from the outlet) is a stone wall with a large round opening. This used to house a pipe to vent train smoke out of the valley.

•The machinery that remains at the top of the dam controlled water flow through a sluiceway. The original Friends Mill, a complex of paper and grist mills, was here.

•The trail bears right through Lock 17, which was the downstream end of a series of four locks needed to maneuver the elevation drop.

•You're now biking in a ravine of the old canal bed. In May this segment of trail is lined with trillium. It's also an active beaver area.

•Pass another cement whistle sign on the right.

•The cement wall in the water is the end of a race from Milo Mills. The stagnant water on the left is the raceway. From here to Penn Yan was the most industrialized section of the outlet.

•A large brick chimney towers over the remains of a paper mill, built in 1890, burned in 1910, and then rebuilt. You can still see the 17-foot flywheel which used two miles of hemp cable and was run by a steam engine. The machinery was manufactured at the Rochester foundry at Brown's Race.

•Cross Milo Mill Road.

•Cross a bridge over a wood-lined sluice. This used to carry water to Shutt's Mill, which dates back to about 1850.

•A small side path immediately to the left leads to the ruins of Shutt's Mill. You can still see the stone vats from this paper mill which manufactured wall board. Shutt's Mill burned in 1933. The first mill at this site was a sawmill built in 1812. It was followed by a wool mill, a gristmill, and a fulling mill. Beware of the poison ivy in the area.

•The waterfall on the far side of the outlet, just before a road and bridge, is outflow from the municipal sewage plant.

•Cross a road. Dibbles Mill used to make wooden wheels in this area.

•The green shed across the road on the right was a blacksmith shop from canal times (around 1838). The blacksmith specialized in shoeing mules.

•Cross paved Fox Mill Road. If you take a left on Fox Mill Road, then a quick right toward the outlet, you'll find remains from the Fox Mill which manufactured straw paper. The stone for the walls was moved here from the dismantled locks of Crooked Lake Canal around 1865.

•Pass a sign for St. John's Mill. Other than the sign, there's nothing to see. The mill used to be across the outlet.

•Cross paved Cherry Street, at 5.5 miles.

•The trail becomes paved.

•Pass under a railroad trestle called "High Bridge." It was originally built of wood in 1850 and was rebuilt in 1890.

•The large circular hollow just after the trestle was once a turntable for the train.

•Pass signs for an exercise trail. After the chin-up bars on the right, a small path leads left to another cement railroad marker "D6" indicating 6 miles from Dresden.

•Reach the wooden bridge, which served as a railroad trestle to Birkett Mills in 1824. Birkett Mills took their water turbines out in 1947.
•Pass under the Main Street (Penn Yan) bridge, built in 1884 from canal stone. This area used to have the guardhouse for the canal. The dam on the right is used to control water level in Keuka Lake. The brown building you can see was a grain warehouse. At one time this section of trail was home to several woodworking factories, a cooperage, and a sash-and-blind factory.
•Pass through a park.
•Cross the pedestrian bridge over the outlet.
•Continue through Penn Yan Recreation Complex on the paved path. You pass restrooms, a boat launch, tennis courts, and a small playground.
•Cross another wooden bridge over Sucker Brook.
•Pass through the athletic fields to the parking lot in Marsh Development Project on Route 54A.
•Turn around and retrace your path.

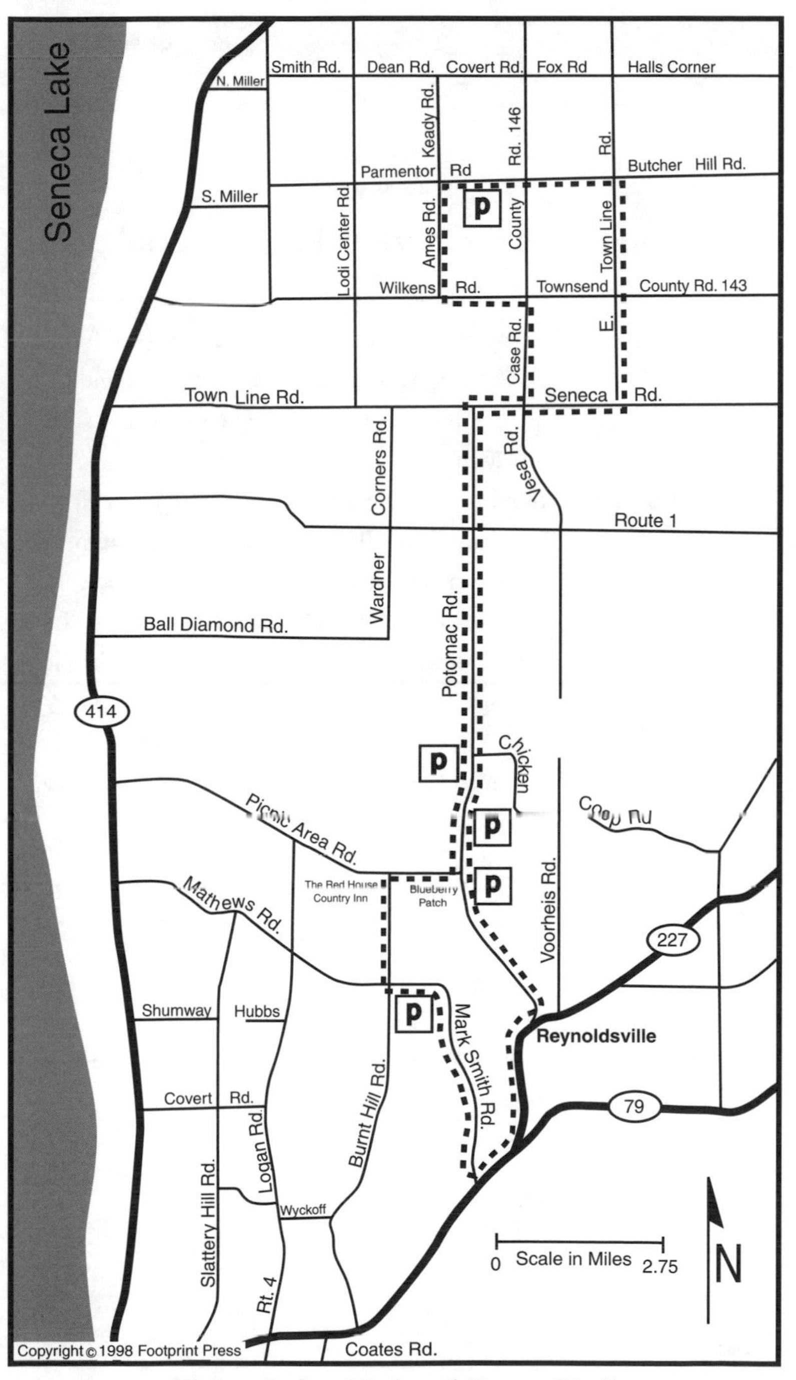

Finger Lakes National Forest Trail

22.

Finger Lakes National Forest Trail

Location: Between Seneca and Cayuga Lakes (south of Seneca Army Depot), about an hour and forty-five minutes by car from downtown Rochester.

Parking: Interloken Trail parking lot on Parmentor Road (Take Route 96A south along the eastern side of Seneca Lake, through Ovid and Lodi. Just past Lodi, turn south onto Keady Road. Take the third left onto Parmentor Road. The parking lot is on the right.)

Alternative Parking: Foster Pond parking on Potomac Road
Potomac Group Campground on Potomac Road
Intersection of Potomac Road and Picnic Area Road
South Pasture parking on Mathews Road
Ravine Trail parking on Picnic Area Road

Riding Time: 4.5 hours

Length: 25.1-mile loop

Difficulty: Difficult, interspersed level areas and steep hills

Surface: Mostly packed dirt roads, some paved roads

Trail Markings: None

Uses:

Finger Lakes National Forest Trail

Contact: Finger Lakes National Forest
5218 State Road 414
Hector, NY 14841-9707
(607) 546-4470

The Finger Lakes National Forest encompasses 16,000 acres of land and has over 30 miles of interconnecting hiking trails. The trails are not open to bicycles. The forest is, however, crisscrossed by a network of single-lane dirt roads which are excellent for biking. These roads are open April 1 through November 30 only. Because the national forest is open to hunting, biking during hunting season is not recommended.

From a bicycle you can explore the deep forests and steep hills of this beautiful countryside. The forest contains a five-acre blueberry patch. What better treat on any bike excursion than devouring a handful of freshly picked blueberries. August and September are the best months to find ripe blueberries. This forest also offers overnight camping and has a privately owned bed-and-breakfast, making it a perfect weekend getaway. Contact the Finger Lakes National Forest for additional information on hiking trails and camping.

Wild turkeys are becoming very common in the fields around the Finger Lakes National Forest.

The area around the Finger Lakes National Forest was originally inhabited by the Iroquois Indians, though little is known of their use of the region. In 1790 the area was divided into 600-acre military lots and distributed among Revolutionary War veterans as payment for their services. These early settlers cleared the land for production of hay and small grains such as buckwheat. As New York City grew, a strong market for these products developed, encouraging more intensive agriculture. The farmers prospered until the middle of the nineteenth century, when a series of unfortunate events occurred: the popularity of motorized transportation in urban centers (reducing the number of horses to be fed), gradual depletion of the soil resource, and competition from midwestern agriculture.

Between 1890 and the Great Depression, over a million acres of farmland were abandoned in south-central New York State. In the 1930s it was obvious that farmers in many parts of the country could no longer make a living from their exhausted land. Environmental damage worsened as they cultivated the land more and more intensively to make ends meet. Several pieces of legislation were passed, including the Emergency Relief Act of 1933, and the Bankhead-Jones Farm Tenant Act of 1937, to address these problems. A new government agency, the Resettlement Administration, was formed to carry out the new laws. This agency not only directed the relocation of farmers to better land or other jobs but also the purchase of marginal farmland by the federal government.

Between 1938 and 1941 over 100 farms were purchased in the Finger Lakes National Forest area and administered by the Soil Conservation Service. Because this was done on a willing-seller, willing-buyer basis, the resulting federal ownership resembled a patchwork quilt. The land was named the Hector Land Use Area and was managed to stabilize the soil by planting conifers and developing a grazing program. Individual livestock owners were

allowed to graze animals on the pastureland in order to show how less intensive agriculture could still make productive use of the land.

By the 1950s many of the objectives of the Hector Land Use Area had been met, and the public was becoming interested in the concept of multiple uses of public land. In 1954 administration responsibilities were transferred to the U.S. Forest Service. In 1985 the name was changed to the Hector Ranger District, Finger Lakes National Forest.

Today this National Forest is used for recreation, hunting, forestry, grazing of private livestock, preservation of wildlife habitat, and education and research. It is a treasure available for all of us to enjoy.

Lodging: Red House Country Inn B&B, Picnic Area Road, (607) 546-8566

Distance between major roads:

Parmentor Rd. parking lot to E. Townline Rd.	1.6 miles
E. Townline Road to Seneca Road	1.9 miles
Seneca Road to Potomac Road	1.0 mile
Potomac Road to Route 227	5.5 miles
Route 227 to Route 79	2.8 miles
Route 79 to Mark Smith Road	0.4 mile
Mark Smith Road to Mathews Road	1.8 miles
Mathews Road to Burnt Hill Road	0.6 mile
Burnt Hill Road to Picnic Area Road	1.6 miles
Picnic Area Road to Potomac Road	0.8 mile
Potomac Road to Seneca Road	4.0 miles
Seneca Road to County Road 146	0.1 mile
County Road 146 to Townsend Road	0.9 mile
Townsend Road to Ames Road	0.9 mile
Ames Road to Parmentor Road	1.0 mile
Parmentor Road to parking lot	0.3 mile

Trail Directions

- From the Interloken Trail parking lot, head east on Parmentor Road. In 0.6 mile you pass Case Road/County Road 146. Continue straight, heading downhill for 1.0 mile on the dirt road, which changed its name to Butcher Hill Road.
- At E. Townline Road turn right (S) onto this dirt road. It is paved in front of houses.
- Pass County Road 143, then turn right (W) onto Seneca Road.
- Follow Seneca Road for 1.0 mile passing Vesa Road and County Road 146/Case Road. At the stop sign, turn left (S) onto Potomac Road. This is a dirt road with rolling hills.
- After 1.0 mile there is a stop sign and a Ballard Pasture sign as you approach paved Route 1. Continue straight (S).
- Pass a "Horse Crossing" sign. The terrain levels out. Two miles from Route 1 is a parking lot for the Backbone Trail and Foster Pond. Chicken Coop Road heads to the east. Continue straight.
- Pass the parking lot for Potomac Group Campground. The dirt road curves southwest and heads downhill.
- Continue south past Picnic Area Road and another parking area.
- Pass a National Forest sign, cross a small creek, and a few houses. Potomac Road ends at paved Route 227. You've come 9.4 miles so far.
- Turn right (SW) onto Route 227. Head downhill past a gravel pit and the Hector Town Hall. Continue on Route 227 for 2.8 miles.
- Turn right (W) onto paved Route 79. Travel 0.4 mile more and you are back to dirt roads.
- At Mark Smith Road turn right (N). Pass some houses. Notice the waterfall to your left just before the "Leaving National Forest" sign.
- This is a steep uphill. Pass the Gorge Trail. The road winds back and forth and continues uphill.
- When the road dead ends, turn left onto Mathews Road. Pass the Burnt Hill Trail, South Velie Pasture, and a parking area. A communications tower is to your right.

- Head downhill past a sign for Blueberry Patch and Interloken Trail and a parking area.
- At the stop sign, turn right onto Burnt Hill Road. Pass Ravine Trail. The road roller-coasters as it heads north. At the next stop sign, you've come 16.6 miles.
- Turn right onto Picnic Area Road. Head uphill past Backbone and Interloken Trails. The Red House Country Inn B&B is on your left. Straight ahead is Backbone Horse Camp.
- At the Blueberry Patch Campground, you may want to take a side trip to pick blueberries if they're in season.
- Pass the Burnt Hill Trail parking area. Pass North Velie Pasture.
- Turn left and head north on Potomac Road. For 4.0 miles you're retracing a route you took earlier heading south. Pass Chicken Coop Road and Route 1.
- At the stop sign at Seneca Road turn right.
- Take the first left onto Case Road/County Road 146.
- In 0.9 mile turn left onto Townsend Road/County Road 143. Only 2.2 more miles and you're done.
- Take the first right (N) onto Ames Road, which is a narrow dirt road. Pass Interloken Trail.
- Turn right and head east on Parmentor Road. The parking lot is on your right in 0.3 mile.

Rides Southwest of Rochester

Genesee Valley Greenway

The Genesee Valley Greenway is a 90-mile historic and natural-resource corridor that follows a transportation route once used by the Genesee Valley Canal, from 1840 to 1878, and later by the railroad, from 1880 to the mid 1960s. The former rail bed now serves as a multi-use greenway trail open to hikers, bikers, horseback riders, cross-country skiers, and snowmobilers. Currently 40 miles of the total 90 miles are open for use. Each year more segments are opened. Three segments are described below.

The trail will eventually connect with the Rochester River Trail, the Erie Canalway Trail, the Finger Lakes Trail, as well as Rochester's Genesee Valley Park and Letchworth State Park.

The Genesee Valley Greenway passes through wetlands, woodlands, rolling farm lands, steep gorges, historic villages, and the Genesee and Black River valleys. It offers something for everyone from a short ride to a challenging long-distance trek. You can stop to explore quaint villages, visit a historic canal-era inn, or inspect well-preserved stone locks and other remnants of the ingenuity and engineering that built the canal and the railroad.

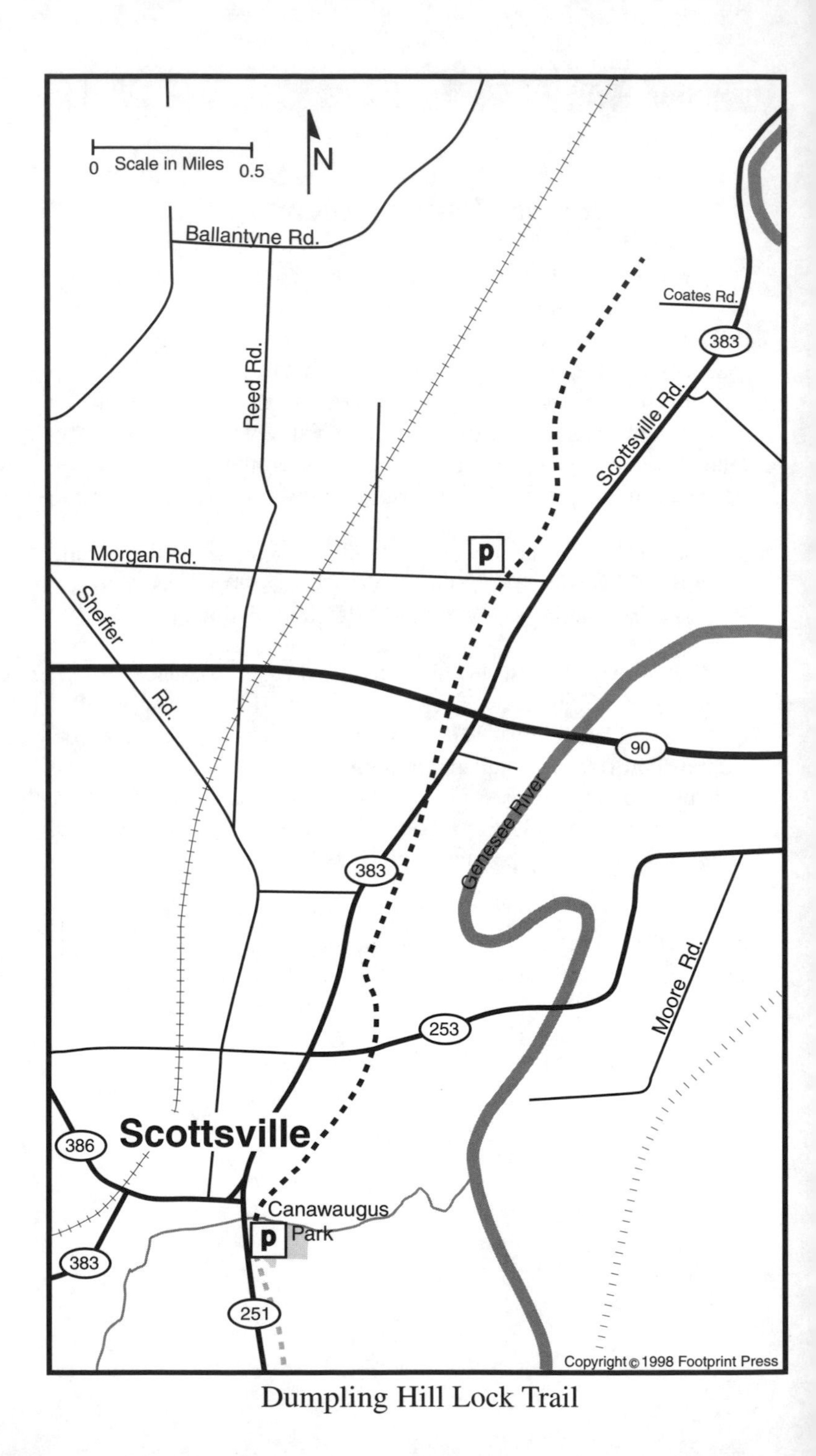

Dumpling Hill Lock Trail

23.

Dumpling Hill Lock Trail

Location: Canawaugus Park (south of the village of Scottsville, Route 251) to Morgan Road, Scottsville (off Route 383)

Parking: Canawaugus Park (south of the village of Scottsville, Route 251) parking lot

Alternative Parking: Trail intersection on Morgan Road

Riding Time: 1 hour one way

Length: 5.1 miles one way

Difficulty: Easy, level

Surface: Cinder path

Trail Markings: None (expected summer 1998)

Uses:

Contact: Friends of the Genesee Valley Greenway, Inc.
16 Chapel Street
Mount Morris, NY 14510
(716) 658-2569

This portion of the greenway trail has a destination in mind. It takes you to Lock 2, the Dumpling Hill Lock, one of the best preserved locks on the Genesee Valley Canal that operated from 1840 to 1878. The canal's original 115 locks were made of either wood, a combination of wood and stone, or all stone. Over the years the wood rotted and most locks deteriorated or were lost altogether. But this 90-foot-long, 15-foot-wide lock is all stone and well preserved. Each lock had a lock keeper and sometimes a lock house. The Dumpling Hill Lock had a house which was located west of the canal near Coates Road.

From the parking area at Canawaugus Park, look across to the north side of Oatka Creek to see an old feeder gate for the Genesee Valley Canal. A feeder gate consisted of a lock, dam, and toll house. If you need to fuel up, before or after your ride, stop for a bite to eat in one of Scottsville's diners.

Lodging: Doubling Hills Inn, 2262 Scottsville Road, Scottsville, (716) 234-7878

Trail Directions

•Begin by crossing Oatka Creek on the plate girder (former Pennsylvania Railroad bridge) known locally as the "George Bridge." You are heading northeast on the trail.
•Cross Route 253 and pass Rodney Farms, a thoroughbred horse farm, on the right.
•At Route 383 bear left as a mowed path leads up to the road.
•Cross the road with care, being certain that you can see oncoming traffic far enough ahead for a safe crossing.
•Turn right, following the shoulder of Route 383.
•On the left side is a small graveyard with the gravestone of Joseph Morgan, a Revolutionary War captain. He is credited with being the first settler in Chili in 1792.
•Watch for the trail on the left heading back into the woods. Lift your bike over the guardrail and head downhill.
•Pass under the New York State Thruway.
•Cross a gravel driveway.
•Cross Morgan Road.
•Pass under two sets of power lines.
•Cross a farm lane, then a second and a third lane.
•The lock is just ahead after the third farm lane.
•Retrace your steps back to Canawaugus Park.

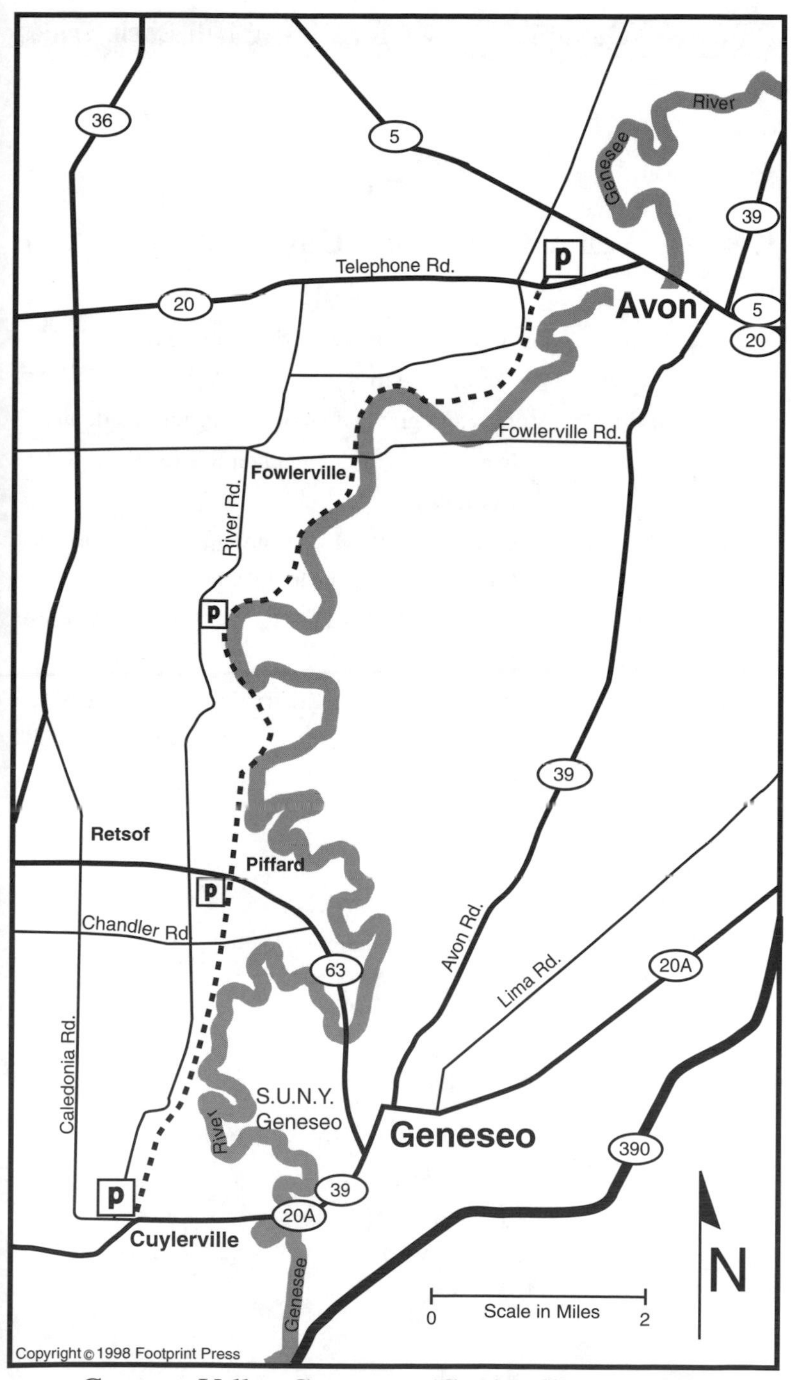

Genesee Valley Greenway (Cuylerville to Avon)

24.

Genesee Valley Greenway (Cuylerville to Avon)

Location: Just north of Mount Morris, running from Cuylerville to Avon

Parking: A grass and gravel area on the northern side of Route 39, near the bend on Route 39 in Cuylerville

Alternative Parking: Yard of Ale Canal House Inn, 3226 Genesee Street (Route 63 near Flats Road)

At the end of York Landing Road, a side road off River Road

Route 20 (Telephone Road), 0.9 mile west of where Routes 5 and 20 split (west of Avon)

Riding Time: 2 hours one way

Length: 12.6 miles one way

Difficulty: Moderate

Surface: Crushed stone, mowed grass, packed dirt

Trail Markings: None (expected summer 1998)

Uses:

Contact: Friends of the Genesee Valley Greenway, Inc.
16 Chapel Street
Mount Morris, NY 14510
(716) 658-2569

Forget your preconception of a converted railroad trail. On this segment you're in for some pleasant surprises. Rather than proceeding straight as an arrow, the trail meanders to follow the sweeping curves of the Genesee River. And, it's not particularly flat. Not that it's hilly, but it does have lots of little hills and dales, which make the ride interesting. The bed is well packed, so that this off-road trail is fairly easy to pedal.

It's hard to match the views along here in the spring and summer. But give it a try when the trees are bare in order to get the full view of the winding Genesee River and the dramatic eroded gorges as water rushes to the river. You'll even pass remains of the cut-stone Lock 5 and several ponds that originally served as turning basins for the Genesee Valley Canal.

The Genesee River begins its northward journey as a small stream in a farmer's field in Pennsylvania and flows 147 miles to Lake Ontario. Native Americans fished the river's waters and traveled its length by canoe. Early settlers used its power to grind grain into flour and to saw trees into lumber. Later, industrial mills harnessed the power to forge iron into parts and weave cotton into cloth. Today the river is a source of recreation and beauty, and its power is still used to generate electricity. The dam at Mount Morris manages the flow of this important waterway.

This country ramble takes you past fields of many varieties, lots of farm lanes, and plenty of wild animals. We got spectacular, close-up looks at a coyote and a fox, as well as the more mundane squirrels, cows, horses, geese, deer, and even a cat.

As you bike along, note the presence of stately old oak trees standing right in the middle of a number of farm fields. Years ago, red oak and shag-bark hickory were the dominant trees in the forests of upstate New York. But, by the early 1900s the forest cover was down to ten percent of its original level, as farmers cleared land for fields and harvested the lucrative lumber. A few oaks were spared.

Their broad canopy provided shade for farmers and their animals as they toiled in the fields. Some of these old oaks are over 200 years old.

This public trail is ours to enjoy thanks to the Friends of the Genesee Valley Greenway, the Department of Environmental Conservation, and New York State Office of Parks, Recreation, and Historic Preservation (OPRHP).

Distance between parking areas:

Route 39 to Route 63	3.8 miles
Route 63 to River Road	2.9 miles
River Road to Route 20	5.9 miles

Trail Directions

•From the Route 39 parking lot, head north along the trail bed.
•Pass a large swamp pond in 0.6 mile.
•Cross a bridge over a creek feeding the Genesee River at 1.2 miles.
•Cross Chandler Road at 3.1 miles. The area to your left was once a Tuscarora Indian village called O-HA-GI.
•At 3.8 miles cross Route 63. Parking is available at the Yard Of Ale Restaurant which serves lunches and dinners daily.
•Further on, Salt Creek flows through a culvert under the rail bed.
•At 6.7 miles pass a pond on the left, then a parking area at the end of a side road off River Road.
•Several times culverts divert water under the rail bed as creek water makes its way to the river.
•Cross Fowlerville Road. You've come 9.3 miles.
•At 10.7 miles the remains of Lock 5, built about 1840, are on the left.
•The trail jogs to the left at a farm lane.
•The trail ends at the parking lot on the northern side of Route 20.

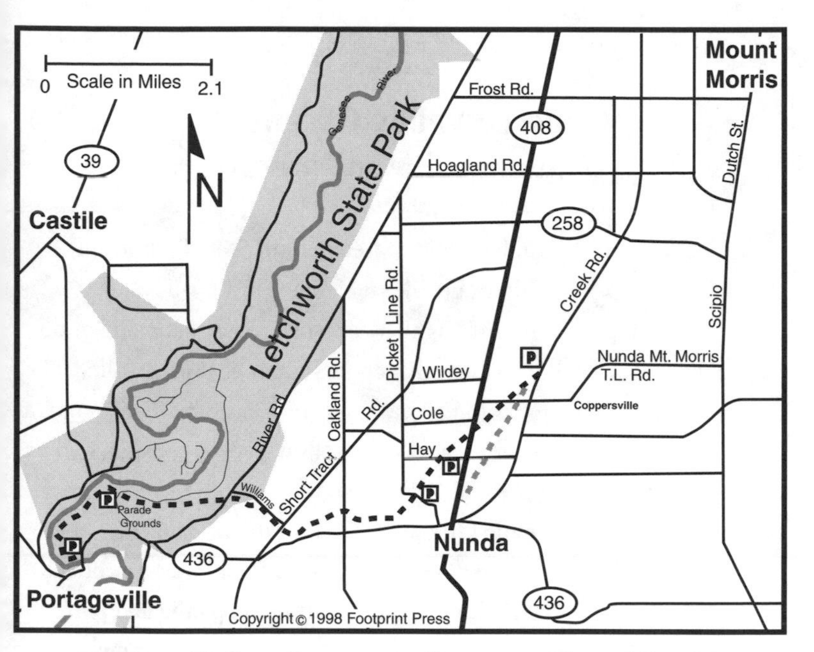

Genesee Valley Greenway (Portageville to Nunda)

25.

Genesee Valley Greenway (Portageville to Nunda)

Location:	Southern end of Letchworth State Park, from Portageville to Nunda
Parking:	Park off Highway 436 on the northern side of the Genesee River, just north of Portageville. The parking area has a "Finger Lakes Trail" sign, a large black-and-yellow pedestrian sign, and a "Road Closed" sign.
Alternative Parking:	Parade Grounds. Turn north off Route 436 at the sign "Letchworth State Park Parade Grounds." Parking is on the left in the picnic and playground area. The trail is a short distance down the road. Restrooms are available.
	Picket Line Road
	Creek Road just north of Coopersville. There is a small white sign set back from the road.
Riding Time:	1.5 hours one way
Length:	9.9 miles one way
Difficulty:	Difficult, some very steep hills, some narrow trail
Surface:	Dirt trail, mowed grass, and packed gravel
Trail Markings:	Yellow blazes on the western portion; green "Genesee Valley Greenway" signs on the eastern portion.

Uses: 

(The portion located in Letchworth State Park is open for biking from June 1 to October 1.)

Contact: Friends of the Genesee Valley Greenway, Inc.
16 Chapel Street
Mount Morris, NY 14510
(716) 658-2569

New York State Office of Parks, Recreation and Historic Preservation
Western District - Genesee Region
One Letchworth State Park
Castile, NY 14427-1124
(716) 493-3600

This challenging, but highly rewarding, trail is located about an hour south of Rochester near Letchworth State Park. The adventure begins with the drive south along Interstate 390. As you head into the Genesee Valley, a panorama of patchwork farms and forests spreads before you. Route 436 parallels the original location of the Genesee Valley Canal. From 1852 until 1877, 17 locks lifted this canal over the hill from Nunda to Portageville. As you drive west on Route 436, be on the lookout to the north for the many stone locks which lie in ruins today.

The trail begins north of Portageville, parallel to the Genesee River on the Finger Lakes Trail. It's a narrow path uphill, then a steep downhill. Once over the hill, you pick up the old railroad bed. This section of the trail is blessed with a series of waterfalls along the Genesee River as well as creeks feeding into the river. The views are spectacular at any time of the year.

You'll be riding within the Genesee River gorge. The railroad was abandoned because of difficulty in keeping the route open. It was often blocked by landslides down the steep banks. Even though the railroad is gone, nature has continued her erosive ways. Landslides have wiped out the original rail bed so that the path becomes narrow, winding, and steep until you reach the Parade Grounds. This section of trail is best suited to mountain bikes.

The Parade Grounds is a picnic and playground area in Letchworth State Park, off Route 436. During the Civil War it was an actual infantry parade grounds. From this point eastward, the trail is a wide, abandoned rail bed, though it continues to be a bit rougher than most converted rail beds. Biking is allowed on this trail from June 1 through October 1. Please don't ride this trail in wet conditions to ensure that it remains open for bicycling.

You can avoid the roughest portion of the ride by starting at the Parade Grounds and heading to the east. But, you'll also miss the most spectacular scenery. If you choose to do this, consider walking 0.5 mile west from the Parade Grounds to see the waterfalls as part of your outing.

A railroad trestle towers overhead as it crosses the Genesee River.

Another option is to ride the Nunda loop. Near the eastern end of the trail is a spur into the town of Nunda (see the map). Begin by heading southwest from the Creek Road parking lot. Bear left when the rail bed diverges. When you reach Route 408 in Nunda, head west until you pick up the trail again on Picket Line Road. Follow the trail northeast back to the Creek Road parking lot. This is about a 3-mile loop.

Other biking paths are available in Letchworth State Park. Write to the New York State Office of Parks, Recreation and Historic Preservation at the address above for a map and information. The park also offers "Bike-Hike" programs.

NOTE: On the southern end of this trail, within Letchworth State Park, biking is allowed on a trial basis. The policy will be reevaluated in 1999, and biking could be eliminated in this section. Please obey all posted regulations to assure that this trail stays open for all to enjoy.

Lodging:
- Glen Iris Inn, 7 Letchworth State Park, Castile, NY 14427, (716) 493-2622, also a restaurant serving three meals daily
- Camping and cabins are available at Letchworth State Park, (800) 456-2267
- Brown's Butternut Bed and Breakfast, Nunda, (716) 468-2805
- Broman's Genesee Falls Inn, corner of Main and Hamilton Streets, Portageville, (716) 493-2484

Bike Shop: Swain Ski and Sports, 131 Main Street, Geneseo. Bike rentals, (800) 836-8460

Distance between roads:

Route 436 to Parade Grounds	2.4 miles
Parade Grounds to Picket Line Road	5.0 miles
Picket Line Road to Creek Road	2.5 miles

Trail Directions

- From the parking area on Route 436, head uphill (SW) toward the "Road Closed" sign. The trail is narrow and marked with the yellow blazes of the Finger Lakes Trail.
- Continue following the yellow blazes as the trail bears left toward the top of the hill. The wide trail to the right is an abandoned road which continues uphill to the active railroad tracks.
- The trail heads downhill.
- At the bottom of the hill turn right onto the railroad bed. (The railroad bed to the left travels for 0.1 mile to the Genesee River where the bridge is out.)
- The wet ditch to your right is the former Genesee Valley Canal.
- Ride under the tall metal railroad trestle. This is Portage High bridge which still carries several freight trains daily. The metal structure replaced the wooden bridge when it burned.
- Notice the waterfall (upper falls) in the river just beyond the trestle.
- The trail becomes narrow and rough as it winds through a landslide area.
- Climb two flights of log stairs, then over a series of waterbars.
- Look behind toward the roaring sound to see the middle falls in the river.
- At 1.9 miles you reach a wide area with a red sign that says "Danger slide area. Keep off." Turn right onto the railroad bed again.
- As you proceed down the rail bed, watch toward the river. If you look west down the river, you can see a cascade of two major waterfalls. Across the river, DEH-GA-YA-SOH Creek tumbles down the gorge bank to join the river. You can easily see why it's called Inspiration Falls!
- At 2.4 miles cross the paved Parade Grounds road. The Parade Grounds parking area is just up the road to your right.
- At 4.2 miles pass a green gate then cross a dirt road (River Road). The Finger Lakes Trail heads off to the left. Be sure to stay on the wide rail bed, do not follow the yellow blazes from this point east.

- At 4.8 miles you come to another dirt road (Williams Road). The rail bed continues straight but is flooded by a beaver dam and is impassable not far beyond. Turn left and follow Williams Road.
- At 5.3 miles cross Short Tract Road and continue straight, again on the rail bed.
- Notice the old canal lock on your right at 5.9 miles. These were composite locks whose sides were lined with wood. Some of the original wood members are still visible.
- Head downhill and cross Oakland Road.
- Jog to the right to continue on the rail bed across the road.
- Head uphill on the trail past the Genesee Valley Greenway sign.
- At 7.4 miles cross Picket Line Road. Parking is available here.
- At 8.0 miles cross Hay Road.
- Cross Route 408 after 8.5 miles.
- At the golf course, stay on the marked trail as you skirt close to the clubhouse. Pass the first tee and a driving range. The rail trail continues on a straight course but you have to make a slight detour to avoid riding directly through the golfers. The entrance back to the rail bed is narrow and rough.
- At 9.3 miles cross Cooperville Road.
- Cross a creek on a wooden bridge. Reach Nunda Junction where the trail to Nunda heads off to the right. Bear left.
- End at the parking area on Creek Road.

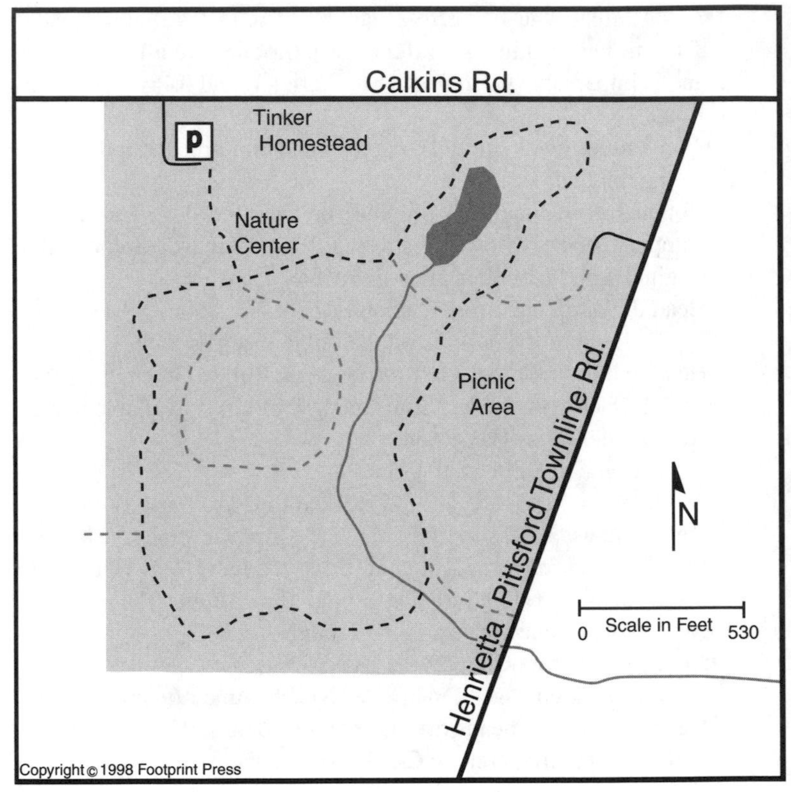

Hansen Nature Center Trail

26.

Hansen Nature Center Trail

Location: 1525 Calkins Road, Henrietta (between Pinnacle Road and Henrietta-Pittsford Townline Road)

Parking: Parking lot at Hansen Nature Center, 1525 Calkins Road

Riding Time: 20 minutes

Length: 1.2-mile loop

Difficulty: Easy, mostly level

Surface: Gravel path

Trail Markings: None

Uses:

(pets are not allowed)

Contact: Hansen Nature Center
1525 Calkins Road
P.O. Box 999
Henrietta, NY 14467-0999
(716) 359-7044
Tinker Museum (716) 359-7042

Donated by the Aldridge family in 1991 and made public in 1994, Tinker Nature Park has become a year-round favorite for all ages. The park consists of woods, wetland, ponds, and fields which together create a living museum of natural history. Within the park is the Hansen Nature Center, offering classes in cross-country skiing, snowshoeing, photography, wildflowers, songbirds, etc. While there, you will also want to visit the Tinker Homestead built in 1830.

This cobblestone museum is free and open to the public on Tuesday, Wednesday, Thursday, Saturday, and Sunday 11 a.m. to 3 p.m. It can be opened for groups and at other times by appointment.

Trail Directions

- From the parking lot follow the paved path past the nature center.
- Bear left. (Trail from the right is a boardwalk offering a nice view of a pond.)
- Continue following the gravel path past a pavilion and picnic area. (The boardwalk shortcut rejoins trail.)
- Bear right where a side trail enters from the road.
- Wind through woods reemerging in a meadow near the nature center.
- Follow the paved path back to parking lot.

Erie Canalway Trail

Erie Canalway Trail

Location: Palmyra to Lockport

Length: 85 miles

Difficulty: Easy, mostly flat

Surface: Paved (asphalt) and packed cinder

Trail Markings: Posts with round metal signs (brown, yellow, and blue) with a packet boat in the center and the words "Erie Canalway Trail" around the perimeter. No signs most of the way.

Uses: 

Contact: New York State Thruway Authority
200 Southern Boulevard
Albany, N.Y. 12209
(514) 436-3034
(800) 4CANAL4

Officially called the Erie Canalway Trail but more commonly known as the towpath, this trail stretches from Palmyra west to Lockport along the Erie Canal. It covers 85 miles and passes four working locks along its route.

The 363-mile Erie Canal was opened with great ceremony in 1825. Dubbed variously "The Grand Canal," "Clinton's Folly," "Clinton's Ditch," and "The Big Ditch," the Erie Canal has been recognized as one of the great engineering feats of its day. With little technical knowledge or precedent to guide them, workers surveyed, blasted, and dug across New York State. They hewed through the hardest of solid rock, dug in infested marshes, devised and erected aqueducts to carry the canal across interrupting valleys and rivers, and constructed 83 locks to carry vessels through the

variations in water height – one great set of locks rising as high as the majestic falls of Niagara.

By connecting the Atlantic Ocean and the Great Lakes, the Erie Canal opened the West and initiated a great surge of commerce. Many communities that sprang up along the new canal still carry their "port" names today, such as Lockport, Brockport, Spencerport, and Fairport. The canal was widened, deepened, and rerouted over the years. In 1917 the enhanced canal was called the Barge Canal. Those were the glorious days of life at a snail's pace as horses and mules towed boats along the canal at four miles per hour taking just under six days to make the trip from Albany to Buffalo. The packet boats, dandy drivers with stovepipe hats, mule teams, and "hoggee" mule drivers are long gone. Today the Erie Canal and its towpath are used almost exclusively for recreation.

Although the towpath is a long trail, you can ride it in chunks of various lengths. A truly enjoyable way to cover the entire length is by making it a several-day trip and staying overnight at the bed-and-breakfasts along the way. As a weekend getaway, park your car along the towpath, pedal out in a single direction, stay in a bed-and-breakfast overnight, and pedal back to your car the next day. What a treat!

The towpath may be long, but it's one of the easiest trails to follow. When in doubt, just choose a path close to the canal. On one side, you're likely to see boats; both recreational and tour boats regularly ply these waters during the summer months. On the other side, you'll probably see trains; in many places active railroad tracks parallel the towpath. Lots to look at!

To present more manageable adventures, we've split the Erie Canalway Trail into the following four segments, traveling east to west:

- Palmyra to Pittsford (trail #27)
- Pittsford to Spencerport (trail #28)
- Spencerport to Albion (trail #29)
- Albion to Lockport (trail #30)

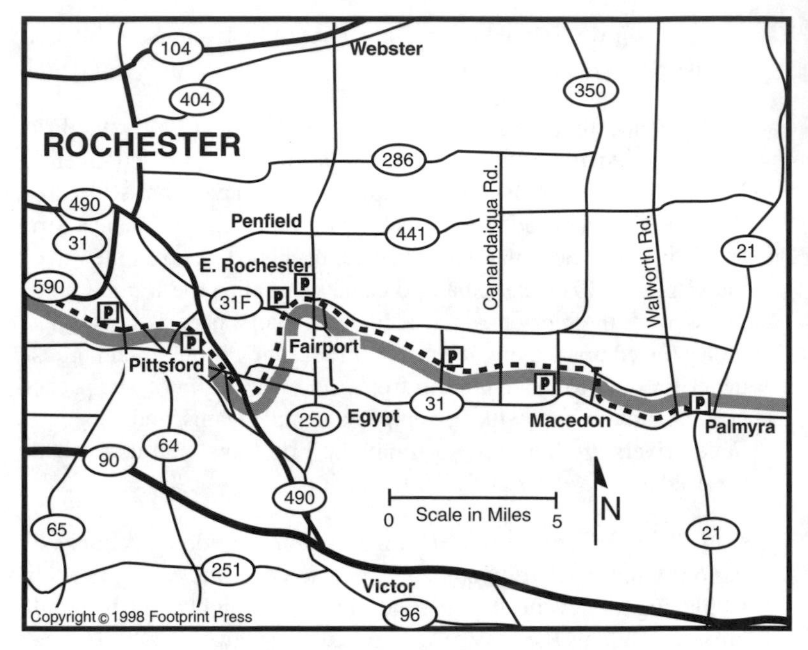

Erie Canalway Trail (Palmyra to Pittsford)

27.

Erie Canalway Trail (Palmyra to Pittsford)

Parking:	Aqueduct Park on the north side of Route 31, just west of the village of Palmyra. Watch for the sign "Lock 29."
Alternative Parking:	Lock 30 on Route 350 in Macedon Wayneport Road, Macedon Village lot behind Riki's Restaurant on Main Street, Fairport Perinton Park on Fairport Road, Fairport Behind Burgundy Basin Inn on Marsh Road, Fairport. Village parking, next to the Coal Tower Restaurant, on Schoen Place, Pittsford
Riding Time:	2.5 hours one way
Length:	18.0 miles one way
Difficulty:	Easy, mostly flat
Surface:	Paved (asphalt) and packed cinder
Trail Markings:	Posts with round metal signs (brown, yellow, and blue) with a packet boat in the center and the words "Erie Canalway Trail" around the perimeter
Uses:	

Distances between parking areas:

Aqueduct Park to Lock 30	3.1 miles
Lock 30 to Wayneport Road	3.3 miles
Wayneport Road to Main Street	4.7 miles
Main Street to Perinton Park	0.8 mile
Perinton Park to Marsh Road	3.3 miles
Marsh Road to Schoen Place	2.8 miles

Palmyra

Settled in 1789 by John Swift, this area was originally called Swift's Landing. Joseph Smith founded the Mormon Church here in 1830. Visitors by the thousands now converge on Palmyra each July for the Mormon's Hill Cumorah pageant, the largest outdoor religious extravaganza in the United States.

The existing Erie Canal flows through Palmyra's historic Aqueduct Park, named for the remnant of an aqueduct from the original Erie Canal which carried water over Ganargua Creek. The home of Lock 29, Aqueduct Park offers campsites, picnic tables, swing sets, a small boat launch, restrooms, and parking. The park is open from 9 a.m. to 9 p.m.

From Aqueduct Park, the trail continues east as a dirt path for 0.7 mile to Church Street/Maple Road. There is no parking available at this terminus.

Bike shop: Palmyra Bike and Scout Shop, 220 E. Main Street, (315) 597-9192

Trail Directions

- From Aqueduct Park, head west on the packed gravel path near the entrance to the park.
- Immediately ride over the aqueduct.
- Head uphill to cross Walworth Road.

- At 2.1 miles, McDonald's and West Wayne Restaurant are across Route 31 to your left.

Macedon

Macedon is the home of the first working lock you'll encounter on this journey, Lock 30. Also, nestled between the current canal and the Mobil Chemical plant, you can explore Lock 61, which was built in 1842. The nearby railroad tracks are from the old New York Central Railroad.

Just after Macedon, the canal widens in several places where they dug the new canal alongside the old one.

Trail Directions

- Head uphill as you approach Quaker Road.
- Turn right and follow the sidewalk across the bridge, then take an immediate left to pick up the towpath. Notice the old canal lock immediately on your right.
  (Side Trip: Follow the short path to your left to old Lock 61 from the 1862 Erie Canal.)
- Ride under pipes which carry materials from the Tenneco (Mobil Chemical) factory to the railroad cars.
- Ride under Route 350 to Lock 30. There's parking on both sides of the canal at Lock 30.
- Cross Canandaigua Road. You've ridden 4.2 miles.
- The canal widens where the old and new canals merged.
- Cross Wayneport Road. There is a small parking lot here.
- At 8.6 miles ride under the old Lyndon Road bridge. This bridge is closed to traffic.
- Just before reaching the Perinton Department of Public Works building, the path becomes paved. For a short section, the path is shared with cars.

Just east of the village of Fairport, active train lines run parallel to the Canalway Trail.

Fairport

It's no exaggeration to say that Fairport owes its existence to the Erie Canal. Much of the area that is now Fairport was once a large swamp. Workers drained it while digging the canal, leaving fertile land instead of swampy ground. Farming prospered, and other businesses quickly sprouted along the canal to carry the harvest to Rochester and New York City.

Fairport boasts the only sloping liftbridge along the Erie Canal. The bridge-tender's tower now houses modern computer equipment to control the bridge's movements.

Lodging:	B&B Introductions, 19 Countryside Road (off Ayrault Road), (716) 383-1166
Bike Shop:	Recreational Vehicles & Equipment, 40 N. Main Street, (716) 388-1350
Tours:	Fairport Lady Paddlewheel Tour Boat, 10 Liftbridge Lane, (716) 223-1930
	Colonial Belle Canal Tour and Dinner Boat, 6 N. Main Street, (716) 377-4600

Trail Directions

- At 10.1 miles a cement bridge abutment with colorful graffiti across the canal signals the terminus of the Perinton Hikeway/Bikeway Trail (trail #11).
- Continue straight and ride under the Turkhill Road bridge.
- Ride under Parker Street.
- On the right, just before the liftbridge is the Box Factory, which contains Lickety Splits Ice Cream Shop and the Village Café Restaurant. Fairport village also has several other restaurants including donut and pizza shops.
- Ride under the sloping liftbridge on Main Street. Walk your bike up a short flight of stairs. You've come 11 miles.
- Ride through the edge of the village lot behind Riki's Restaurant on Main Street. Parking is available here.
- Pass Liftbridge Rentals (renting canoes, kayaks, and bikes) and the headquarters of the tour boat Fairport Lady.
- Pass the American Can Company with its name spelled out in brick on the tall smokestack. It started life as the Sanitary Can Company in 1881.
- Ride under Fairport Road (Route 31F). You've come 12.0 miles
- At 12.2 miles the paving stops, and the trail reverts to packed gravel.
- On the far side of the canal is a wide water, locally known as the oxbow, formed when the canal was enlarged and water levels rose. The island in front of the oxbow is the artificial result of many years of dredging.
- Ride under Ayrault Road.
- Ride under Pittsford-Palmyra Road (Route 31).
- At 14.5 miles pass guard gate #10.
- Ride under Interstate 490.

Bushnell's Basin

In the early 1820s, before the Great Embankment was completed, Hartwell's Basin was the western terminal of the canal. After the full canal opened, William Bushnell operated a fleet of canal boats from the area, and the name was eventually changed to Bushnell's Basin. In its heyday, the port at Bushnell's Basin was a major shipper of agricultural products and a stop for the Rochester, Syracuse, and Eastern Trolley line on its route between Rochester and Canandaigua. Richardson's Canal Inn started life as a hotel on the canal and trolley line.

The 80-foot-high embankment was built to span the Irondequoit Valley. Irondequoit Creek now runs through a tunnel under the canal. Two metal guard gates stand at either end of the embankment.

Lodging: Oliver Loud's Country Inn, 1474 Marsh Road,
Pittsford, (716) 248-5200
(across the canal via Marsh Road)

Trail Directions

- Traverse the great embankment with its cement walls rising 70 feet above the Irondequoit Valley below.
- Across the canal are Richardson's Canal House and Oliver Loud's Country Inn. They were a hotel, tavern, and stagecoach stop dating back to the early 1800s.
- Pass concrete abutments used to carry the Inter-Urban Trolley from Canandaigua to Rochester.
- Ride under Marsh Road bridge at 15.1 miles. Across the Marsh Road bridge and to the right is Abbott's Ice Cream and Pontillo's Pizza.
- Parking is available behind Burgundy Basin Inn on Marsh Road.
- Pass Great Embankment Park with a dock, boat launch, and parking.
- Pass a guard gate at 16.8 miles.
- Ride under the Mitchell Road bridge.
- Ride under State Street (Route 31) bridge. The path again becomes paved. Across the canal is Oak Creek Canoes (canoe rental).
- Schoen Place is on your right with restaurants (Marie's White Thumb Bakery and Café, Aladdins, Coal Tower), an ice cream

The Sam Patch stops at Pittsford to pick up passengers for Erie Canal cruises.

shop (Bill Wahl's), and a bicycle shop (Towpath Bike Shop). Village parking is available next to the Coal Tower Restaurant on Schoen Place. Please walk your bike through this congested section.

Pittsford

Pittsford was a thriving village well before the Erie Canal arrived. The big spring was used by the Iroquois Indians as a stopover point on their trade route through the area. The canal, even today, draws its water from the spring.

Originally called Northfield, this town claimed Monroe County's first school, first library, first lawyer, and first physician. The name was changed to Pittsford in 1814.

A grain mill, which still operates on Schoen Place along the canal, attracted a wide variety of ducks. They have interbred to form some unusual combinations and now stay on the canal year round. It's tempting to feed the ducks, but please avoid the temptation. Feeding encourages large numbers of them to stay in close proximity. As a result of this unnatural congregation, a plague is spreading through their ranks.

Pittsford is home to Locks 32 and 33.

Bike Shop: Towpath Bike Shop, 7 Schoen Place, (716) 381-2808
Tours: Sam Patch Tour Boat, 12 Cornhill Terrace (stops at Schoen Place), (716) 262-5661

Ducks live year round in the canal waters in Pittsford.

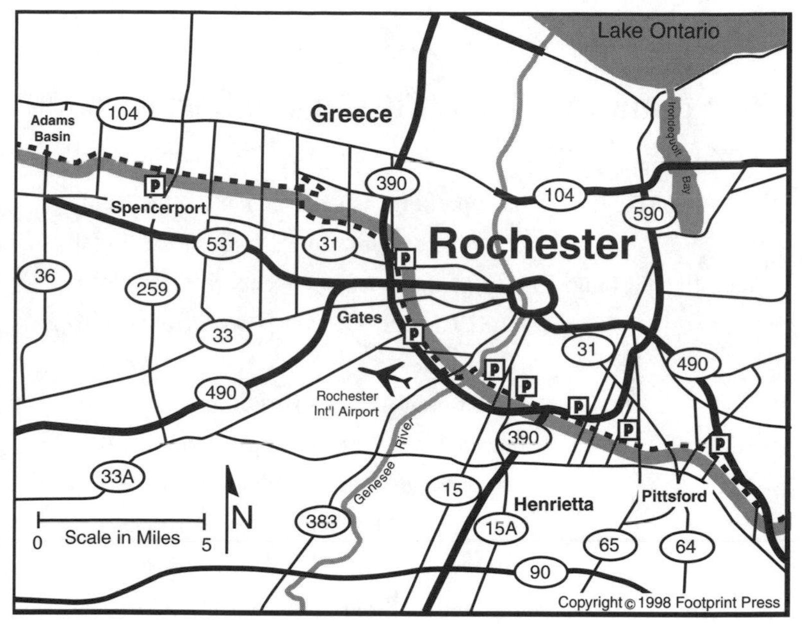

Erie Canalway Trail (Pittsford to Spencerport)

28.

Erie Canalway Trail (Pittsford to Spencerport)

Parking: Village parking is available next to the Coal Tower Restaurant on Schoen Place, Pittsford

Alternative Parking: Lock 32 Canal Park, Clover Street, Pittsford
Lock 33 Canal Park, Edgewood Avenue, Henrietta
South Clinton Avenue, Brighton
Brighton Town Park, Westfall Road, Brighton
Genesee Valley Park off Moore Drive, Rochester
Holiday Inn, 911 Brooks Avenue, Rochester
Lyell Avenue (Route 31), Rochester
Union Street (Route 259), Spencerport

Riding Time: 3.25 hours one way

Length: 19.1 miles one way

Difficulty: Easy, mostly flat

Surface: Paved (asphalt) and packed gravel

Trail Markings: None

Uses:

Distances between parking areas:

Schoen Place to Lock 32 Canal Park	1.7 miles
Lock 32 Canal Park to Lock 33 Canal Park	1.3 miles
Lock 33 Canal Park to South Clinton Avenue	1.7 miles
South Clinton Avenue to Brighton Town Park	0.6 mile

Brighton Town Park to Genesee Valley Park	2.1 miles
Genesee Valley Park to Holiday Inn	1.7 miles
Holiday Inn to Lyell Avenue	2.7 miles
Lyell Avenue to Union Street	7.8 miles

Rochester

The Erie Canal turned Rochesterville into a boomtown. Today it's the third largest city in New York State. The first Erie Canal traveled through the center of the city, across an 800-foot stone aqueduct. The second, sturdier version was built in 1842 and is now the base of the Broad Street bridge. When the canal was widened and deepened into the Barge Canal, its route was redirected south of Rochester to its current location.

Locks 32 and 33 in this next section are the only locks on the system that are narrower at the bottom than at the top. No one really knows why they were built this way. However, as a result, barges that were tied side by side in the canal were squeezed as they descended. The two locks are close together, and in the days of heavy traffic, lockfulls of water had to be dumped from Lock 33 to prevent flooding of the surrounding area. To alleviate the problem, a large surge pool was excavated on the northern bank.

You'll pass through Genesee Valley Park on your way through the outskirts of Rochester. The trail takes you past four arched bridges; the third one crosses the Genesee River, another very important waterway in western New York State.

Lodging: Holiday Inn Airport, 911 Brooks Avenue,
(716) 328-6000

Trail Directions

•From Schoen Place, head west on the towpath along the canal.
•Ride under the Main Street (Pittsford) bridge.
•Ride under an active railroad bridge.

•Ride under the Monroe Avenue bridge.
•Follow the canal-trail signs and turn right at the NYS Canal Maintenance property.
•Turn left onto Brook Road.
•Bear left at the yellow metal gate to complete the detour around the NYS Canal Maintenance property and return uphill to the towpath along the canal.
•1.4 miles from Schoen Place, pass the Historic Erie Canal and Railroad Loop Trail heading off to your right. (See trail #12)
•Ride under the Clover Street (Route 65) bridge and uphill to Lock 32 and the Lock 32 Canal Park. Parking is available here.
•Cross a causeway over the mouth of the surge pool.
•At 2.8 miles pass the Jewish Community Center on your right.
•Ride under Edgewood Avenue.
•Carry your bike up some stairs to Henrietta Lock 33. This is the last lock for 65 miles until Lockport.
•Ride under Winton Road.
•Ride under South Clinton Avenue. You've come 4.7 miles.
•Ride under the twin bridges of Interstate 390 twice.
•Pass Brighton Town Park with parking.
•Ride under East Henrietta Road (Route 15A).
•Ride under West Henrietta Road (Route 15).
•Ride under Kendrick Road. You've come 6.6 miles.
•Pass two guard gates. These, and the set west of the Genesee River, protect the canal against any severe water level changes from the river.
•Pass two sets of abandoned railroad tracks.
•Head downhill under Moore Drive in Genesee Valley Park.
•Pass two of the three gray, stone, arched bridges designed by Frederick Law Olmstead on your left. Red Creek enters the canal between these two bridges on the far side of the canal. Parking is available in Genesee Valley Park.
•Cross the Genesee River on the Waldo J. Nielson bridge. It's the third arched bridge you come to — the one with metal railings.
•Turn left immediately after the bridge.

A tug pushes a barge loaded with trees retrieved from the Genesee River, at the crossroads where the Genesee River and Erie Canal meet.

- •Ride over the arched bridge over the canal (the third bridge built by Olmsted)
- •Turn right before reaching the Interstate 390 bridge.
- •Ride under Scottsville Road (Route 383). You've come 7.7 miles. The Greater Rochester International Airport will be on your left.
- •Pass two guard gates.
- •Pass an old abandoned railroad bridge.
- •Pass the Holiday Inn. Parking is available here.
- •Ride under Brooks Avenue (Route 204). You've come 8.6 miles.
- •Cross the Rochester & Southern Railroad.
- •Cross Chili Avenue (Route 33A). For the next 0.8 mile, the trail is double wide.
- •At 10.1 miles, cross the bridge, high over the Conrail Railroad.
- •Cross Buffalo Road (Route 33).
- •Ride under Interstate 490 twice.

- At 11.3 miles cross Lyell Avenue (Route 31). Parking is available here.
- Ride under Lee Road.

Greece

Greece was a bustling canal town in the 1800s. It had a grocery store, post office, school, and two doctor's offices, all now long gone, but replaced by a town with a population of approximately 90,000.

Trail Directions

- Ride under Interstate 390.
- At 13.3 miles pass under the Long Pond Road bridge. The path turns to gravel.
- At 13.8 miles note Junction Lock on the north side of the canal.
- Enter Allen's Canalside Marina. Follow the driveway out to Elmgrove Road.
- Turn right to cross the canal on the Elmgrove Road (Route 386) bridge.
- After the bridge turn right on Ridgeway Avenue and enter Henpeck Park. Parking is available here. The trail loops under the Elmgrove Road bridge and continues along the north side of the canal.
- Arrive at Greece Canal Park at 15.8 miles.
- Reach Manitou Road (Route 261).
- Ride under Gillet Road at 17.6 miles.
- Pass guard gate 11. A cove on the right was the path of the original Erie Canal.
- Ride parallel to Canal Street.
- This section ends at Union Street (Route 259), Spencerport.

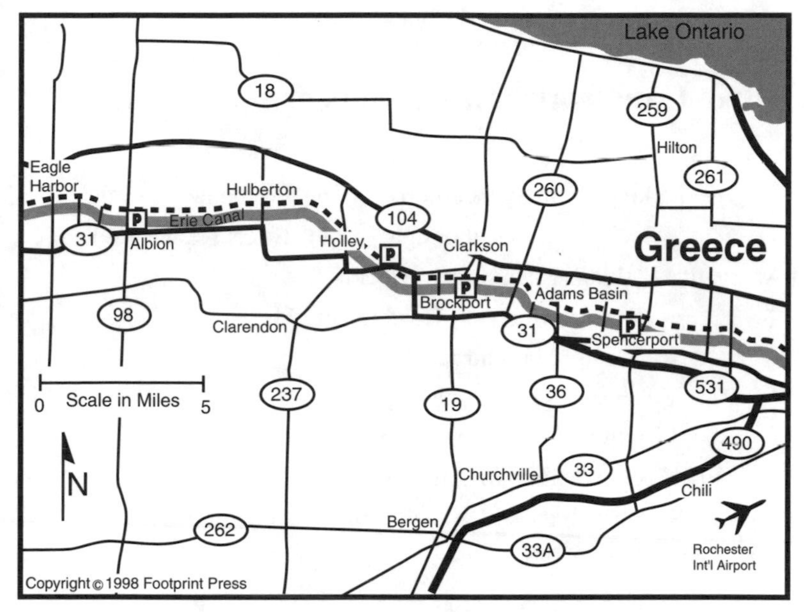

Erie Canalway Trail (Spencerport to Albion)

29.
Erie Canalway Trail (Spencerport to Albion)

Parking:	In Spencerport, park on the south side of the canal or along Union Street (Route 259)
Alternative Parking:	Main Street, Brockport
	Brockport Road (Route 31)
	Main Street, Albion
Riding Time:	4 hours one way
Length:	22.1 miles one way
Difficulty:	Easy, mostly flat
Surface:	Packed gravel, some mowed grass
Trail Markings:	None
Uses:	

Distances between parking areas:

Union Street, Spencerport, to Main Street, Brockport	7.6 miles
Main Street, Brockport, to Route 31	3.1 miles
Route 31 to Main Street, Albion	11.4 miles

Spencerport

The settlement that began as Ogden Center in 1802 became Spencerport in 1825 after the canal was dug through Daniel Spencer's land. The original liftbridge control tower was moved to Pulver House Museum (696 Colby Street) in 1973.

Bike Shop: Sugar's Bike Shop, 2 Slayton Ave., (716) 352-8300 (in a plaza one mile south of the canal)

Trail Directions

- •Cross Union Street (Route 259). A variety of restaurants are located along Union Street south of the bridge. An ice cream parlor in Upton Place in located one block north of the trail.
- •Ride under the Martha Street bridge.
- •Ride under the Trimmer Road bridge.
- •Eventually, the canal widens to a basin on the far side.

Adams Basin

Adams Basin was settled by William Adams and his family from Massachusetts in 1825, after the canal had opened. He built a business around a basin, dry-dock, and warehouse. The Canalside Inn, now a bed-and-breakfast, is reputedly the oldest tavern west of Rochester. The original bar is still in the house and dates back to 1827.

Lodging: Canalside Inn B&B, 425 Washington Street, (716) 352-6784

Trail Directions

- •Cross Washington Street (Route 36). The liftbridge is on your left and the Canalside Inn on your right. The next 0.9 mile is on mowed grass.
- •Parallel a road for 0.2 mile until reaching Gallup Road.
- •Ride under Gallup Road.
- •Ride under Sweden Walker Road (Route 260). You've come 5.4 miles.

Brockport

Brockport, which is located 40 miles west of Palmyra and 45 miles east of Lockport, is the halfway point for the Erie Canalway Trail. Now home to Brockport State University, this town gained fame in 1875 for the Globe Iron Works, which manufactured the first 100 McCormick reapers. The site of the old factory is now

McCormick Park on the canal, near the Park Street bridge. There are lots of restaurants, cafes, and pizza shops in town. Park along Main Street.

Brockport boasts two liftbridges situated just 900 feet apart and operated by one person who dashes from one to the other.

Lodging: Clarkson Corners B&B, 3734 Lake Road North, (716) 637-0340 (1 mile north of the canal)
Portico B&B, 3741 Lake Road North, (716) 637-0220 (0.5 mile north on Route 19)
Victorian B&B, 320 Main Street, (716) 637-7519 (4 blocks south of the canal)
Bike Shop: Towpath Bike Shop, 45 N. Main Street, (716) 637-9901 (one block north of the canal)

Trail Directions

- Cross Fayette Street/Park Avenue next to the liftbridge.
- Cross Main Street (Route 19). Parking is available near this liftbridge.
- Ride under the Smith Street bridge. You've come 8 miles so far.
- Cross a metal grate over a spillway.
- Pass a guard gate.
- Ride under the Redman Road (Route 31) bridge at 9.2 miles.
- Ride under the Brockport Road bridge (Route 31). Parking is available here, off Monroe-Orleans County Line Road.

Holley

Although he had no connection with the area, the village is named after Myron Holley. Mr. Holley was a member of the Canal

Commission responsible for building the original Erie Canal. He is buried at Mount Hope Cemetery in Rochester.

Trail Directions

•Cross East Avenue.
•Ride under the West Holley Road bridge and pass a guard gate.
•Ride under the Telegraph Road bridge.
•Ride under the Groth Road bridge.
•Cross Hulberton Road. This is a liftbridge.
•Ride under Fancher-Brockville Road.
•Ride under Hindsburg Road.
•Ride under Transit Road.
•Ride under Denismore Road.
•Ride under Keitel Road.
•Ride under Butts Road.
•Ride under Brown Street.
•Ride under Ingersoll Street.
•Cross Main Street, Albion. Parking is available on both sides of the canal, near the Main Street bridge.

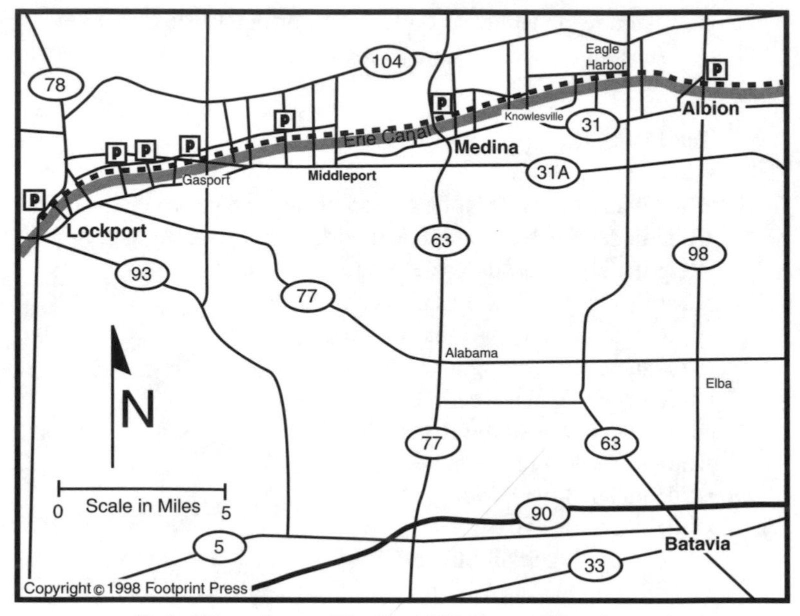

Erie Canalway Trail (Albion to Lockport)

30.

Erie Canalway Trail (Albion to Lockport)

Parking:	Route 98, Albion, on both sides of the canal, near the Main Street bridge.
Alternative Parking:	Route 63, Medina, on the southern side of the canal
	Peet Street
	Orangeport Road
	Day Road
	Cold Springs Road
	Lockport, along streets near the canal
Riding Time:	4 hours one way
Length:	28 miles one way
Difficulty:	Easy, mostly flat
Surface:	Packed gravel, some mowed grass
Trail Markings:	None
Uses:	

Distances between parking areas:

Albion to Medina	11.2 miles
Medina to Peet Street	6.3 miles
Peet Street to Orangeport Road	4.9 miles
Orangeport Road to Day Road	2.8 miles
Day Road to Cold Springs Road	0.9 mile
Cold Springs Road to Lockport	1.9 miles

Albion

Albion is the county seat of Orleans County. The town boasts a Methodist Church dating to 1860, a Presbyterian Church with a spire 175 tall, and a Greek-revival courthouse built in 1857 and located 1/4 mile south of the trail on Main Street (Route 98). Albion was the home of George Pullman, inventor of the Pullman railroad car. Legend has it that he conceived the idea while watching passengers on packet boats along the Erie Canal.

Lodging: Friendship Manor B&B, 349 S. Main Street, (716) 589-2983 (less than a mile south of the canal)

Bike Shop: Sugar's Bike Shop, 26 N. Main Street, (716) 638-8002

Trail Directions

- Cross Main Street, Albion (Route 98). Public parking is available near the canal on both sides of the Main Street bridge.
- Ride under a bridge and past a guard gate.
- Ride under the Gaines Basin Road bridge. You've ridden 1.8 miles.
- Watch for cement walls marking a creek that flows under the canal.
- Cross Waterport Road at Eagle Harbor. You have to carry your bike down a few steps.
- Ride under Allens Bridge Road. You've come 4.1 miles.
- Ride under the Presbyterian Road bridge.
- Eventually, the canal widens.
- Cross Knowlesville Road. This is the 6.4-mile mark.

Medina

Medina grew on fertile land with ideal weather conditions for growing fruit. A curve in the canal made it a natural harbor for hauling produce as well as Medina sandstone. Just east of Medina, off Route 31, Culvert Road passes under the canal. Featured in *Ripley's Believe It Or Not*, it's the only road that passes under the

Erie Canal. Built in 1823, it's an interesting sight and worth the side trip to take a look.

Medina also is home to the Medina Railroad Center. This museum of railroad memorabilia is located in a restored 1905 wood-frame freight house at 530 West Avenue, (716) 798-6106.

Bike Shop: Canalside Bicycle and Fitness Shop, 439 Main Street, (716) 798-4360

Oak Orchard Creek flows under the canal and cascades down a waterfall alongside the Canalway Trail.

Trail Directions

- At 8.0 miles watch for the cement walls in the canal where Culvert Road runs under the canal.
- Ride under Beals Road.
- Cross a road. Follow the trail around the bridge and a new guard gate.
- At 10.5 miles ride under the Bates Road bridge. Oak Orchard Creek runs under the canal here. Look for the waterfall to the

right as you cross the creek, then continue on a cement dike which separates the creek from the canal.
•Ride under Glenwood Avenue.
•Reach downtown Medina at 11.2 miles. Parking is available across the liftbridge.
•Ride under Marshall Road.
•Pass guard gate 16 at 14.4 miles.

Middleport

The Village Variety store sells ice cream.

Lodging: Canal Country Inn, 4021 Peet Street, (716) 735-7572 (on the canal)

Trail Directions
•Cross North Main Street at 16 miles.
•Ride under Carmen Road.
•Ride under the Peet Street bridge. Parking is available here. You've ridden 17.5 miles.

Gasport/Orangeport

Bike Shop: B&G Bikes, 7549 Ridge Road, Gasport, (716) 772-2448

Trail Directions
•Ride under a bridge.
•Ride under Slayton Settlement Road bridge.
•Cross a metal grate bridge over a spillway at 20.5 miles.
•Pass a new guard gate.
•Cross Main Street, Gasport at 21.3 miles.
•Ride under Orangeport Road. Parking is available here.
•Ride under Canal Road.
•Ride under Day Road. You've come 25.2 miles. Parking is available here.
•Ride under Cold Springs Road. Parking is available. The Widewaters Marina and Canal Park are visible across the canal.

Lockport

The trail ends at a flight of two locks, Locks 34 and 35. This is where the canal climbs 50 feet up the Niagara Escarpment. Ahead and to the right are the original "Famous Five" stair locks, now relegated to water overflow. On the original canal, these five paired locks allowed simultaneous travel in either direction. One flight was replaced by the modern two-step locks which operate today. Straight ahead is the old hydraulic power house, which supplied electricity to operate the locks and liftbridges. Today it's the New York State Erie Canal Museum, a great place to learn more of the canal's history. There are lots of restaurants in downtown Lockport.

Lodging: Hambleton House B&B, 130 Pine Street, 14094, (716) 439-9507 (two blocks south of the canal)
Bike Shop: Freewheelers Cycle and Fitness, 5891 S. Transit Road, (716) 434-9036 (in plaza above Lock 35)
Tours: Lockport Locks and Canal Tours, P.O. Box 1197, 14095, (716) 693-3260

Trail Directions

- Ride under the Matt Murphy Way bridge. You're 1.3 miles from the end.
- Cross Adams Street. There is a liftbridge here.
- Cross Exchange Street. This liftbridge is closed to traffic. Only 0.7 mile to go.
- Turn right through a brown gate and follow the trail around a maintenance area. Notice the dry dock inside the fenced area.
- Pass the remains of a pulp mill and old power plant to the right. The 2,430 foot-long raceway tunnel was built in 1858.
- Ride under the railroad bridge. Notice the Erie Canal Museum ahead.
- Pass Locks 34 and 35 as the path takes you up the Niagara Escarpment and under a bridge. The path ends here. Parking is available along the streets near the locks. Be sure not to park in the spaces reserved for senior citizens visiting the community center near by.

References:

Finger Lakes Trail Conference, Inc.
202 Colebourne Road
Rochester, NY 14609-6733
e-mail fltc@axsnet.com
(716) 288-7191

Genesee Valley Cycling Club
Neil J. Rowe
57 S. Beacon Hills Drive
Penfield, NY 14526

Rails-to-Trails Conservancy
1400 Sixteenth Street NW, Suite 300
Washington, DC 20036
(202) 797-5400

Rochester Bicycling Club, Inc.
P.O. Box 10100
Rochester, NY 14610-0100
(716) 723-2953
http://www.win.net/~rbcbbs

Western New York Mountain Biking Association
P.O. Box 1691
Amherst, NY 14226-7691

Web Sites

Visit these web sites for bike specs, prices, and lots of other useful information.

The World Wide Bicycle Tour Directory..........www.bicycletour.com
Adventure Sports..................................www.adventuresports.com
Rochester Outdoors.. www.maxlent.com
Yahoo Cycling.............www.yahoo.com/Recreation/Sports/Cycling
Great Outdoor Recreation Page....www.gorp.com/gorp/activity/biking
Upstate NY Biking Clubs...............www.win.net/~rbcbbs/links.htm
Friends of Webster Trails........ www.frontiernet.net/nbaird/friends.htm

Bike Manufacturers' Web Sites:
Barracuda Bike Company.................................... www.tomclark.com
Bianchi Bicycles ....www.bianchi.com
Bontrager Bikes..www.bontrager.com
Boulder Bikes...www.boulderbikes.com
Breezer Bikes...............................www.earthpledge.org/mall/breezer
Cannondale Bikes.......................................www.cannondale.com
Carumba Bikes..www.caramba.com
Diamondback Bicycles..............................www.diamondback.com
Ellsworth Bicycles.............................www.ellsworthbicycles.com
Gary Fisher Bicycles...................................... www.fisherbikes.com
GT Bicycles...www.gtbicycles.com
Girvin Bikes..www.girvin.com
Ibis Cycles...www.ibiscycles.com
Kestrel Bikes...www.kestrel-usa.com
Klein Bikes..www.kleinbikes.com
Kona Bikes..........................www.konaworld.com/Kcntrlcntr.html
Litespeed Titanium Bicycles.................................www.litespeed.com
Marin Mountain Bikes....................................www. marinbikes.com
Merlin Bikes...www.merlinbike.com
Mountain Cycle...www.mountaincycle
Orange Cycle.......................www.cyclenet.co.uk/orange/index.html
Performance Bicycle...............................www.performancebike.com

Pro-Flex Bikes..www.cruztel.com/proflex
Raleigh Bicycles..www.raleighbikes.com
Salsa Cycles..www.salsacycles.com
Santa Cruz Bicycles..www.santacruzmtb.com
Schwinn Bicycles..www.schwinn.com
Softride..www.softride.com
Specialized Bicycles..www.specialized.com
Titus Titanium Bicycles..www.titusti.com
Trek Bicycles..www.sportsite.com
Ventana Mountain Bikes..www.ventanausa.com
VooDoo Cycles..www.voodoo-cycles.com

Definitions:

Aqueduct: A structure that carries a canal across another body of water. The Rochester aqueduct (now Broad Street in downtown), spanned the Genesee River for over 800 feet, and was the largest in the world.

Carding: Combing of wool.

Fulling mill: A mill for cleaning wool and producing cloth.

Gristmill: A mill for grinding grain into flour.

Guard gate: A large metal partition used as a safeguard when lowered against high water surges, dike leaks, or to lower water for canal repairs.

Hoggee: A mule driver who was paid pitifully low wages to drive mules along the Erie Canal.

Mule: The sterile offspring of a male donkey and a female horse

Sawmill: A mill for cutting trees into lumber.

Towpath: A path used for towing boats along a canal. The Erie Canal towpath is now the Erie Canalway Trail.

Weir: A dam in a stream used to raise the water level or divert its flow.

Trails Under 5 Miles

Page	Trail Name	Length (miles)
163	Hanson Nature Center Trail	1.2
61	North Ponds Park Trail	1.3
91	Electric Trolley Trail	1.8
95	Cartersville - Great Embankment Loop Trail	2.4
38	Genesee Valley Park Loop Trail	2.6
108	Victor - Lehigh Valley Rail Trail	2.8
121	Ontario Pathways Trail	3.4
56	Webster - Hojack Trail	3.5
117	Canadice Lake Trail	3.7
82	Perinton Hikeway/Bikeway	4.4
50	Mount Hope Cemetery	any

Trails 5 to 10 Miles

Page	Trail Name	Length (miles)
32	Greece Interstate 390 Trail	5.0
149	Dumpling Hill Lock Trail	5.1
77	Canal Park Trailway	5.8
86	Historic Erie Canal and Railroad Loop Trail	6.0
64	Webster - Route 104 Trail	6.1
127	Middlesex Valley Railroad Trail	6.8
43	Genesee River - Downtown Loop Trail	7.0
74	Hannibal Hojack Rail Trail	7.4
100	Auburn Trail	7.5
132	Keuka Lake Outlet Trail	7.5
156	Genesee Valley Greenway (Portageville)	9.9
50	Mount Hope Cemetery	any

Trails Over 10 Miles

Page	Trail Name	Length (miles)
111	Mendon - Lehigh Valley Rail Trail	12.5
152	Genesee Valley Greenway (Cuylerville)	12.6
68	Cayuga County Trail	13.0
50	Mount Hope Cemetery	14.5
168	Erie Canalway Trail (Palmyra to Pittsford)	18.0
176	Erie Canalway Trail (Pittsford to Spencerport)	19.1
182	Erie Canalway Trail (Spencerport to Albion)	22.1
140	Finger Lakes National Forest Trail	25.1
186	Erie Canalway Trail (Albion to Lockport)	28.0

Combination Trails

Page	Trail Name	Length (miles)
38 & 43	Genesee Valley Park Loop Trail & Genesee River - Downtown Loop Trail	9.6
43 & 176	Genesee River - Downtown Loop Trail & Erie Canalway Trail (Pittsford to Spencerport)	7.0+
61 & 64	North Ponds Park Trail &Webster - Route 104 Trail	7.4+
86 & 168 or 176	Historic Erie Canal and Railroad Loop Trail & Erie Canalway Trail	6.0+
91 & 168 or 176	Electric Trolley Trail & Erie Canalway Trail	2.0+
108 & 111	Victor - Lehigh Valley Rail Trail & Mendon - Lehigh Valley Rail Trail	15.3
100 & 108 & 111	Auburn Trail & Victor - Lehigh Valley Rail Trail & Mendon - Lehigh Valley Rail Trail	21.8
168-191	4 segments of the Erie Canalway Trail	85.0

Loop Trails

Page	Trail Name	Length (miles)
163	Hanson Nature Center Trail	1.2
61	North Ponds Park Trail	1.3
91	Electric Trolley Trail	1.8
95	Cartersville - Great Embankment Loop Trail	2.4
38	Genesee Valley Park Loop Trail	2.6
86	Historic Erie Canal and Railroad Loop Trail	6.0
43	Genesee River - Downtown Loop Trail	7.0
140	Finger Lakes National Forest Trail	25.1
50	Mount Hope Cemetery	any

Easy Trails

Page	Trail Name	Length (miles)
163	Hanson Nature Center Trail	1.2
61	North Ponds Park Trail	1.3
91	Electric Trolley Trail	1.8
38	Genesee Valley Park Loop Trail	2.6
108	Victor - Lehigh Valley Rail Trail	2.8
121	Ontario Pathways Trail	3.4
117	Canadice Lake Trail	3.7
82	Perinton Hikeway/Bikeway	4.4
32	Greece Interstate 390 Trail	5.0
149	Dumpling Hill Lock Trail	5.1
86	Historic Erie Canal and Railroad Loop Trail	6.0
64	Webster - Route 104 Trail	6.1
43	Genesee River - Downtown Loop Trail	7.0
74	Hannibal Hojack Rail Trail	7.4
100	Auburn Trail	7.5
132	Keuka Lake Outlet Trail	7.5
68	Cayuga County Trail	13.0
168	Erie Canalway Trail (Palmyra to Pittsford)	18.0
176	Erie Canalway Trail (Pittsford to Spencerport)	19.1
182	Erie Canalway Trail (Spencerport to Albion)	22.1
186	Erie Canalway Trail (Albion to Lockport)	28.0

Moderate Trails

Page	Trail Name	Length (miles)
95	Cartersville - Great Embankment Loop Trail	2.4
56	Webster - Hojack Trail	3.5
77	Canal Park Trailway	5.8
127	Middlesex Valley Railroad Trail	6.8
152	Genesee Valley Greenway (Cuylerville to Avon)	12.6
50	Mount Hope Cemetery	any

Difficult Trails

Page	Trail Name	Length (miles)
156	Genesee Valley Greenway (Portageville)	9.9
111	Mendon - Lehigh Valley Rail Trail	12.5
140	Finger Lakes National Forest Trail	25.1

Word Index

C

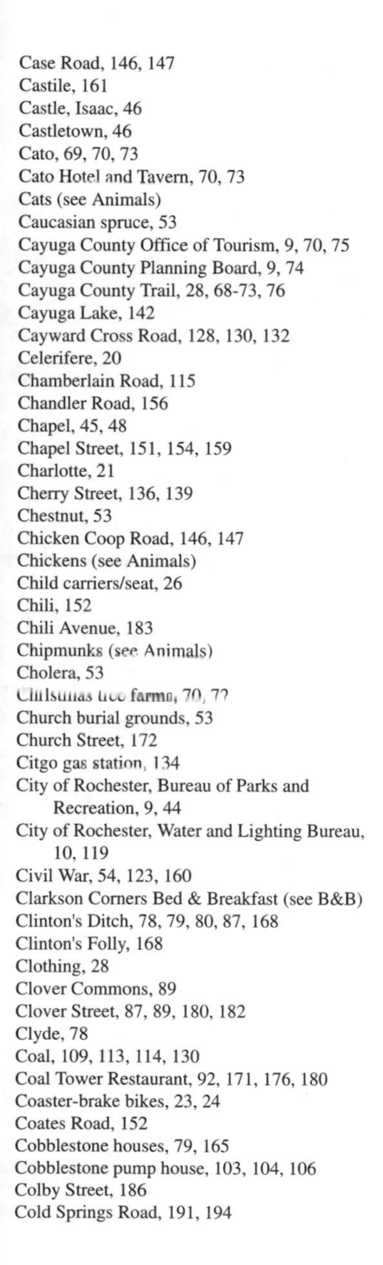

D

Word Index

Other Books Available from Footprint Press

Take a Hike! Family Walks in the Rochester Area

A practical guide to exploring Rochester, NY's 40+ trails and interesting places. Through maps and descriptions this book shows where to take a stroll, walk the dog, or expose your kids to nature while having fun and learning local history.
ISBN # 0-9656974-6-0 US $16.95 Can $21.95

Bruce Trail, An Adventure Along the Niagara Escarpment

Come along as experienced backpackers take you on a five week, 465 mile journey over the rocky spine of the Niagara Escarpement in Ontario, Canada. As an armchair traveler or in preparation for a hike of your own, you'll enjoy this ramble along a truly unique part of North America.
ISBN # 0-9656974-3-6 US $16.95 Can $21.95

Alter, A Simple Path to Emotional Wellness

Alter is a self-help workbook which assists in recognizing and changing your emotional blocks and limiting belief systems. It uses easy to learn techniques of biofeedback to retrieve subliminal information and achieve personal transformation.
ISBN # 0-9656974-8-7 US $16.95 Can $21.95

For more information explore our web site at:
www.footprintpress.com

Yes, I'd like to order Footprint Press books:

#

____ ***Take A Hike!*** *Family Walks in the Rochester Area*

____ ***Take Your Bike!*** *Family Rides in the Rochester Area*

____ ***Bruce Trail*** *- An Adventure Along the Niagara Escarpment*

____ ***Alter*** *- A Simple Path to Emotional Wellness*

____ Total Books @ $16.95 US or $21.95 Can. each

For 1 or 2 books, add $3 per book for tax and shipping.
For 3 or more books, **FREE** (tax and shipping will be included in book price)

Total enclosed: $____________

Your Name: ______________________________________

Address: ____

City: ________________ State (Province): ____________

Zip (Postal Code): ______________ Country: __________

Make check payable and mail to:
Footprint Press
P.O. Box 645-R
Fishers, NY 14453

Footprint Press books are available at special discounts when purchased in bulk for sales promotions, premiums, or fundraising.